The Etruscans: A Very Short Introduction

VERY SHORT INTRODUCTIONS are for anyone wanting a stimulating and accessible way into a new subject. They are written by experts, and have been translated into more than 40 different languages.

The Series began in 1995, and now covers a wide variety of topics in every discipline. The VSI library now contains over 350 volumes—a Very Short Introduction to everything from Psychology and Philosophy of Science to American History and Relativity—and continues to grow in every subject area.

Very Short Introductions available now:

ACCOUNTING Christopher Nobes
ADVERTISING Winston Fletcher
AFRICAN HISTORY John Parker and
    Richard Rathbone
AFRICAN RELIGIONS Jacob K. Olupona
AGNOSTICISM Robin Le Poidevin
AMERICAN HISTORY Paul S. Boyer
AMERICAN IMMIGRATION
    David A. Gerber
AMERICAN LEGAL HISTORY
    G. Edward White
AMERICAN POLITICAL PARTIES
    AND ELECTIONS L. Sandy Maisel
AMERICAN POLITICS
    Richard M. Valelly
THE AMERICAN PRESIDENCY
    Charles O. Jones
ANAESTHESIA Aidan O'Donnell
ANARCHISM Colin Ward
ANCIENT EGYPT Ian Shaw
ANCIENT GREECE Paul Cartledge
THE ANCIENT NEAR EAST
    Amanda H. Podany
ANCIENT PHILOSOPHY Julia Annas
ANCIENT WARFARE Harry Sidebottom
ANGELS David Albert Jones
ANGLICANISM Mark Chapman
THE ANGLO-SAXON AGE John Blair
THE ANIMAL KINGDOM
    Peter Holland
ANIMAL RIGHTS David DeGrazia
THE ANTARCTIC Klaus Dodds
ANTISEMITISM Steven Beller
ANXIETY Daniel Freeman and
    Jason Freeman

THE APOCRYPHAL GOSPELS
    Paul Foster
ARCHAEOLOGY Paul Bahn
ARCHITECTURE Andrew Ballantyne
ARISTOCRACY William Doyle
ARISTOTLE Jonathan Barnes
ART HISTORY Dana Arnold
ART THEORY Cynthia Freeland
ASTROBIOLOGY David C. Catling
ATHEISM Julian Baggini
AUGUSTINE Henry Chadwick
AUSTRALIA Kenneth Morgan
AUTISM Uta Frith
THE AVANT GARDE David Cottington
THE AZTECS David Carrasco
BACTERIA Sebastian G. B. Amyes
BARTHES Jonathan Culler
THE BEATS David Sterritt
BEAUTY Roger Scruton
BESTSELLERS John Sutherland
THE BIBLE John Riches
BIBLICAL ARCHAEOLOGY Eric H. Cline
BIOGRAPHY Hermione Lee
THE BLUES Elijah Wald
THE BOOK OF MORMON
    Terryl Givens
BORDERS Alexander C. Diener and
    Joshua Hagen
THE BRAIN Michael O'Shea
THE BRITISH CONSTITUTION
    Martin Loughlin
THE BRITISH EMPIRE Ashley Jackson
BRITISH POLITICS Anthony Wright
BUDDHA Michael Carrithers
BUDDHISM Damien Keown

BUDDHIST ETHICS Damien Keown
CANCER Nicholas James
CAPITALISM James Fulcher
CATHOLICISM Gerald O'Collins
CAUSATION Stephen Mumford and
　Rani Lill Anjum
THE CELL Terence Allen and
　Graham Cowling
THE CELTS Barry Cunliffe
CHAOS Leonard Smith
CHILDREN'S LITERATURE
　Kimberley Reynolds
CHINESE LITERATURE Sabina Knight
CHOICE THEORY Michael Allingham
CHRISTIAN ART Beth Williamson
CHRISTIAN ETHICS D. Stephen Long
CHRISTIANITY Linda Woodhead
CITIZENSHIP Richard Bellamy
CIVIL ENGINEERING David Muir Wood
CLASSICAL LITERATURE William Allan
CLASSICAL MYTHOLOGY
　Helen Morales
CLASSICS Mary Beard and John Henderson
CLAUSEWITZ Michael Howard
CLIMATE Mark Maslin
THE COLD WAR Robert McMahon
COLONIAL AMERICA Alan Taylor
COLONIAL LATIN AMERICAN
　LITERATURE Rolena Adorno
COMEDY Matthew Bevis
COMMUNISM Leslie Holmes
THE COMPUTER Darrel Ince
THE CONQUISTADORS
　Matthew Restall and
　Felipe Fernández-Armesto
CONSCIENCE Paul Strohm
CONSCIOUSNESS Susan Blackmore
CONTEMPORARY ART
　Julian Stallabrass
CONTEMPORARY FICTION
　Robert Eaglestone
CONTINENTAL PHILOSOPHY
　Simon Critchley
COSMOLOGY Peter Coles
CRITICAL THEORY
　Stephen Eric Bronner
THE CRUSADES Christopher Tyerman
CRYPTOGRAPHY Fred Piper and
　Sean Murphy
THE CULTURAL REVOLUTION
　Richard Curt Kraus
DADA AND SURREALISM
　David Hopkins
DARWIN Jonathan Howard
THE DEAD SEA SCROLLS Timothy Lim
DEMOCRACY Bernard Crick
DERRIDA Simon Glendinning
DESCARTES Tom Sorell
DESERTS Nick Middleton
DESIGN John Heskett
DEVELOPMENTAL BIOLOGY
　Lewis Wolpert
THE DEVIL Darren Oldridge
DIASPORA Kevin Kenny
DICTIONARIES Lynda Mugglestone
DINOSAURS David Norman
DIPLOMACY Joseph M. Siracusa
DOCUMENTARY FILM
　Patricia Aufderheide
DREAMING J. Allan Hobson
DRUGS Leslie Iversen
DRUIDS Barry Cunliffe
EARLY MUSIC Thomas Forrest Kelly
THE EARTH Martin Redfern
ECONOMICS Partha Dasgupta
EDUCATION Gary Thomas
EGYPTIAN MYTH Geraldine Pinch
EIGHTEENTH-CENTURY BRITAIN
　Paul Langford
THE ELEMENTS Philip Ball
EMOTION Dylan Evans
EMPIRE Stephen Howe
ENGELS Terrell Carver
ENGINEERING David Blockley
ENGLISH LITERATURE Jonathan Bate
ENTREPRENEURSHIP Paul Westhead
　and Mike Wright
ENVIRONMENTAL ECONOMICS
　Stephen Smith
EPIDEMIOLOGY Rodolfo Saracci
ETHICS Simon Blackburn
ETHNOMUSICOLOGY Timothy Rice
THE ETRUSCANS Christopher Smith
THE EUROPEAN UNION John Pinder
　and Simon Usherwood
EVOLUTION Brian and
　Deborah Charlesworth
EXISTENTIALISM Thomas Flynn
THE EYE Michael Land
FAMILY LAW Jonathan Herring
FASCISM Kevin Passmore
FASHION Rebecca Arnold

FEMINISM Margaret Walters
FILM Michael Wood
FILM MUSIC Kathryn Kalinak
THE FIRST WORLD WAR
    Michael Howard
FOLK MUSIC Mark Slobin
FOOD John Krebs
FORENSIC PSYCHOLOGY David Canter
FORENSIC SCIENCE Jim Fraser
FOSSILS Keith Thomson
FOUCAULT Gary Gutting
FRACTALS Kenneth Falconer
FREE SPEECH Nigel Warburton
FREE WILL Thomas Pink
FRENCH LITERATURE John D. Lyons
THE FRENCH REVOLUTION
    William Doyle
FREUD Anthony Storr
FUNDAMENTALISM Malise Ruthven
GALAXIES John Gribbin
GALILEO Stillman Drake
GAME THEORY Ken Binmore
GANDHI Bhikhu Parekh
GENIUS Andrew Robinson
GEOGRAPHY John Matthews and
    David Herbert
GEOPOLITICS Klaus Dodds
GERMAN LITERATURE Nicholas Boyle
GERMAN PHILOSOPHY Andrew Bowie
GLOBAL CATASTROPHES Bill McGuire
GLOBAL ECONOMIC HISTORY
    Robert C. Allen
GLOBAL WARMING Mark Maslin
GLOBALIZATION Manfred Steger
THE GOTHIC Nick Groom
GOVERNANCE Mark Bevir
THE GREAT DEPRESSION AND THE
    NEW DEAL Eric Rauchway
HABERMAS James Gordon Finlayson
HAPPINESS Daniel M. Haybron
HEGEL Peter Singer
HEIDEGGER Michael Inwood
HERODOTUS Jennifer T. Roberts
HIEROGLYPHS Penelope Wilson
HINDUISM Kim Knott
HISTORY John H. Arnold
THE HISTORY OF ASTRONOMY
    Michael Hoskin
THE HISTORY OF LIFE Michael Benton
THE HISTORY OF MATHEMATICS
    Jacqueline Stedall
THE HISTORY OF MEDICINE
    William Bynum
THE HISTORY OF TIME
    Leofranc Holford-Strevens
HIV/AIDS Alan Whiteside
HOBBES Richard Tuck
HUMAN EVOLUTION Bernard Wood
HUMAN RIGHTS Andrew Clapham
HUMANISM Stephen Law
HUME A. J. Ayer
HUMOUR Noël Carroll
THE ICE AGE Jamie Woodward
IDEOLOGY Michael Freeden
INDIAN PHILOSOPHY Sue Hamilton
INFORMATION Luciano Floridi
INNOVATION Mark Dodgson
    and David Gann
INTELLIGENCE Ian J. Deary
INTERNATIONAL MIGRATION
    Khalid Koser
INTERNATIONAL RELATIONS
    Paul Wilkinson
INTERNATIONAL SECURITY
    Christopher S. Browning
ISLAM Malise Ruthven
ISLAMIC HISTORY Adam Silverstein
ITALIAN LITERATURE Peter Hainsworth
    and David Robey
JESUS Richard Bauckham
JOURNALISM Ian Hargreaves
JUDAISM Norman Solomon
JUNG Anthony Stevens
KABBALAH Joseph Dan
KAFKA Ritchie Robertson
KANT Roger Scruton
KEYNES Robert Skidelsky
KIERKEGAARD Patrick Gardiner
THE KORAN Michael Cook
LANDSCAPE ARCHITECTURE
    Ian H. Thompson
LANDSCAPES AND
    GEOMORPHOLOGY
    Andrew Goudie and Heather Viles
LANGUAGES Stephen R. Anderson
LATE ANTIQUITY Gillian Clark
LAW Raymond Wacks
THE LAWS OF THERMODYNAMICS
    Peter Atkins
LEADERSHIP Keith Grint
LINCOLN Allen C. Guelzo
LINGUISTICS Peter Matthews

LITERARY THEORY Jonathan Culler
LOCKE John Dunn
LOGIC Graham Priest
MACHIAVELLI Quentin Skinner
MADNESS Andrew Scull
MAGIC Owen Davies
MAGNA CARTA Nicholas Vincent
MAGNETISM Stephen Blundell
MALTHUS Donald Winch
MANAGEMENT John Hendry
MAO Delia Davin
MARINE BIOLOGY Philip V. Mladenov
THE MARQUIS DE SADE John Phillips
MARTIN LUTHER Scott H. Hendrix
MARTYRDOM Jolyon Mitchell
MARX Peter Singer
MATHEMATICS Timothy Gowers
THE MEANING OF LIFE
    Terry Eagleton
MEDICAL ETHICS Tony Hope
MEDICAL LAW Charles Foster
MEDIEVAL BRITAIN John Gillingham
    and Ralph A. Griffiths
MEMORY Jonathan K. Foster
METAPHYSICS Stephen Mumford
MICHAEL FARADAY
    Frank A. J. L. James
MICROECONOMICS Avinash Dixit
MODERN ART David Cottington
MODERN CHINA Rana Mitter
MODERN FRANCE
    Vanessa R. Schwartz
MODERN IRELAND Senia Pašeta
MODERN JAPAN
    Christopher Goto-Jones
MODERN LATIN AMERICAN
    LITERATURE
    Roberto González Echevarría
MODERN WAR Richard English
MODERNISM Christopher Butler
MOLECULES Philip Ball
THE MONGOLS Morris Rossabi
MORMONISM Richard Lyman Bushman
MUHAMMAD Jonathan A.C. Brown
MULTICULTURALISM Ali Rattansi
MUSIC Nicholas Cook
MYTH Robert A. Segal
THE NAPOLEONIC WARS
    Mike Rapport
NATIONALISM Steven Grosby
NELSON MANDELA Elleke Boehmer

NEOLIBERALISM Manfred Steger
    and Ravi Roy
NETWORKS Guido Caldarelli and
    Michele Catanzaro
THE NEW TESTAMENT
    Luke Timothy Johnson
THE NEW TESTAMENT AS
    LITERATURE Kyle Keefer
NEWTON Robert Iliffe
NIETZSCHE Michael Tanner
NINETEENTH-CENTURY BRITAIN
    Christopher Harvie and
    H. C. G. Matthew
THE NORMAN CONQUEST
    George Garnett
NORTH AMERICAN INDIANS
    Theda Perdue and Michael D. Green
NORTHERN IRELAND
    Marc Mulholland
NOTHING Frank Close
NUCLEAR POWER Maxwell Irvine
NUCLEAR WEAPONS
    Joseph M. Siracusa
NUMBERS Peter M. Higgins
OBJECTIVITY Stephen Gaukroger
THE OLD TESTAMENT
    Michael D. Coogan
THE ORCHESTRA D. Kern Holoman
ORGANIZATIONS Mary Jo Hatch
PAGANISM Owen Davies
THE PALESTINIAN-ISRAELI
    CONFLICT Martin Bunton
PARTICLE PHYSICS Frank Close
PAUL E. P. Sanders
PENTECOSTALISM William K. Kay
THE PERIODIC TABLE Eric R. Scerri
PHILOSOPHY Edward Craig
PHILOSOPHY OF LAW
    Raymond Wacks
PHILOSOPHY OF SCIENCE
    Samir Okasha
PHOTOGRAPHY Steve Edwards
PHYSICAL CHEMISTRY Peter Atkins
PLAGUE Paul Slack
PLANETS David A. Rothery
PLANTS Timothy Walker
PLATO Julia Annas
POLITICAL PHILOSOPHY
    David Miller
POLITICS Kenneth Minogue
POSTCOLONIALISM Robert Young

POSTMODERNISM Christopher Butler
POSTSTRUCTURALISM
    Catherine Belsey
PREHISTORY Chris Gosden
PRESOCRATIC PHILOSOPHY
    Catherine Osborne
PRIVACY Raymond Wacks
PROBABILITY John Haigh
PROGRESSIVISM Walter Nugent
PROTESTANTISM Mark A. Noll
PSYCHIATRY Tom Burns
PSYCHOLOGY Gillian Butler and
    Freda McManus
PURITANISM Francis J. Bremer
THE QUAKERS Pink Dandelion
QUANTUM THEORY
    John Polkinghorne
RACISM Ali Rattansi
RADIOACTIVITY Claudio Tuniz
RASTAFARI Ennis B. Edmonds
THE REAGAN REVOLUTION Gil Troy
REALITY Jan Westerhoff
THE REFORMATION Peter Marshall
RELATIVITY Russell Stannard
RELIGION IN AMERICA Timothy Beal
THE RENAISSANCE Jerry Brotton
RENAISSANCE ART
    Geraldine A. Johnson
REVOLUTIONS Jack A. Goldstone
RHETORIC Richard Toye
RISK Baruch Fischhoff and John Kadvany
RIVERS Nick Middleton
ROBOTICS Alan Winfield
ROMAN BRITAIN Peter Salway
THE ROMAN EMPIRE
    Christopher Kelly
THE ROMAN REPUBLIC
    David M. Gwynn
ROMANTICISM Michael Ferber
ROUSSEAU Robert Wokler
RUSSELL A. C. Grayling
RUSSIAN HISTORY Geoffrey Hosking
RUSSIAN LITERATURE Catriona Kelly
THE RUSSIAN REVOLUTION
    S. A. Smith
SCHIZOPHRENIA Chris Frith and
    Eve Johnstone
SCHOPENHAUER Christopher Janaway
SCIENCE AND RELIGION
    Thomas Dixon

SCIENCE FICTION David Seed
THE SCIENTIFIC REVOLUTION
    Lawrence M. Principe
SCOTLAND Rab Houston
SEXUALITY Véronique Mottier
SHAKESPEARE Germaine Greer
SIKHISM Eleanor Nesbitt
THE SILK ROAD James A. Millward
SLEEP Steven W. Lockley and
    Russell G. Foster
SOCIAL AND CULTURAL
    ANTHROPOLOGY
    John Monaghan and Peter Just
SOCIALISM Michael Newman
SOCIOLINGUISTICS John Edwards
SOCIOLOGY Steve Bruce
SOCRATES C. C. W. Taylor
THE SOVIET UNION Stephen Lovell
THE SPANISH CIVIL WAR
    Helen Graham
SPANISH LITERATURE Jo Labanyi
SPINOZA Roger Scruton
SPIRITUALITY Philip Sheldrake
STARS Andrew King
STATISTICS David J. Hand
STEM CELLS Jonathan Slack
STUART BRITAIN John Morrill
SUPERCONDUCTIVITY
    Stephen Blundell
SYMMETRY Ian Stewart
TEETH Peter S. Ungar
TERRORISM Charles Townshend
THEOLOGY David F. Ford
THOMAS AQUINAS Fergus Kerr
THOUGHT Tim Bayne
TIBETAN BUDDHISM
    Matthew T. Kapstein
TOCQUEVILLE Harvey C. Mansfield
TRAGEDY Adrian Poole
THE TROJAN WAR Eric H. Cline
TRUST Katherine Hawley
THE TUDORS John Guy
TWENTIETH-CENTURY BRITAIN
    Kenneth O. Morgan
THE UNITED NATIONS
    Jussi M. Hanhimäki
THE U.S. CONGRESS Donald A. Ritchie
THE U.S. SUPREME COURT
    Linda Greenhouse
UTOPIANISM Lyman Tower Sargent

THE VIKINGS Julian Richards
VIRUSES Dorothy H. Crawford
WITCHCRAFT Malcolm Gaskill
WITTGENSTEIN A. C. Grayling
WORK Stephen Fineman

WORLD MUSIC Philip Bohlman
THE WORLD TRADE ORGANIZATION
  Amrita Narlikar
WRITING AND SCRIPT
  Andrew Robinson

Available soon:

NUTRITION David A. Bender
CORAL REEFS Charles Sheppard
COMPLEXITY John H. Holland

HORMONES Martin Luck
ALEXANDER THE GREAT
  Hugh Bowden

For more information visit our website
www.oup.com/vsi/

Christopher Smith

THE ETRUSCANS

A Very Short Introduction

OXFORD
UNIVERSITY PRESS

OXFORD
UNIVERSITY PRESS

Great Clarendon Street, Oxford, OX2 6DP,
United Kingdom

Oxford University Press is a department of the University of Oxford.
It furthers the University's objective of excellence in research, scholarship,
and education by publishing worldwide. Oxford is a registered trade mark of
Oxford University Press in the UK and in certain other countries

Published in the United States of America by Oxford University Press
198 Madison Avenue, New York, NY 10016, United States of America

British Library Cataloguing in Publication Data
Data available

Library of Congress Control Number: 2014930343

ISBN 978-0-19-954791-3

Printed and bound by
CPI Group (UK) Ltd, Croydon, CR0 4YY

Acknowledgements

I was approached to write this book some years ago; I am grateful to OUP and especially Emma Ma for her patience. Fortunately, there was a substantial advantage to my procrastination; between the commission and the writing, I came to the British School at Rome as Director. Without the resources of the BSR, the nearby Villa Giulia, one of the great museums of the world, and the many colleagues who have inspired and helped me here in Italy, this would have been a much poorer account.

It would be impossible to name all those who have generously spent time with me, and in some instances read the text. I do however want specifically to acknowledge for their advice, friendship, and collegiality at key moments Gilda Bartoloni, Maria Cristina Biella, Paolo Bruschetti, Francesco Maria Cifarelli, Giovanni Colonna, Massimiliano di Fazio, Francesco di Gennaro, Daniele Maras, Laura Michetti, Elena Tassi Scandone, Anna Maria Moretti Sgubini, Alessandro Naso, Alfonsina Russo, Mario Torelli, and Andrea Zifferero; Roberta Cascino, Robert Coates-Stephens, Sophie Hay, and Letizia Ceccarelli at the BSR; Guy Bradley, Tim Cornell, Robert Leighton, Corinna Riva, and Simon Stoddart in the UK; and the readers of the press. Susan Smith valiantly helped me write a very short introduction. Any remaining faults are wholly my own.

Contents

List of illustrations xv

Introduction 1

1 The origins of the Etruscans 8

2 The Etruscan language 14

3 Towards the Etruscan city-state 20

4 The Villanovan revolution 25

5 The transformation of Etruria 36

6 Etruscan tomb painting and Etruscan art 53

7 Empire, crisis, and response, 600–300 BC 64

8 Etruscan religion 86

9 The Roman conquest 98

10 Clothing and the Etruscan body 115

11 Imperial epilogue 122

12 Etruscology: its origins and development 131

Further reading 139

Index 145

List of illustrations

1   Map of Italy showing
    Villanovan, Etruscan, and
    Greek settlements **2**

2   Map of Etruria and its
    mineral resources **5**

3   Phoenician, Greek, and Latin
    alphabets **15**

4   Pyrgi tablets **17**
    Courtesy of the Ministero Beni e Att.
    Culturali, photo: Scala, Florence

5   Maps of key Etruscan
    sites **26**

6   A hut urn, from Cerveteri **32**
    Courtesy of the Ministero Beni e Att.
    Culturali, photo: Scala, Florence

7   Wine bowl, made by
    Aristonothos **38**
    DeAgostini Picture Library/Scala,
    Florence

8   A tomb of hunting and
    fishing **44**
    Glow Images

9   Tomba Giglioli Tarquinia **54**
    De Agostini Picture Library/
    The Bridgeman Art Library

10 Bucchero vessels **58**
    (a) Courtesy of the Ministero Beni e
    Att. Culturali, photo: Scala,
    Florence; (b) Scala, Florence

11 Etruscan bronze mirror **61**
    © The Art Gallery Collection/Alamy

12 Pyrgi frieze decoration **84**
    Courtesy of the Ministero Beni e
    Att. Culturali, photo: Scala,
    Florence

13 Piacenza liver **92**
    DeAgostini Picture Library/Scala,
    Florence

14 Laris Pulenas
    sarcophagus **93**
    Glow Images

15 A gold stud, from Borchia di
    Vignanello **116**
    DeAgostini Picture Library/Scala,
    Florence

16 The sarcophagus of Seianti
    Hanunia Tlesnasa **120**

17 The Terme Taurine, near
    Cerveteri **127**

The publisher and the author apologize for any errors or omissions in the above list. If contacted they will be pleased to rectify these at the earliest opportunity.

Introduction

From around 900 to 400 BC, the most innovative, powerful, wealthy, and creative people in Italy were the Etruscans. They lived in the hills and plains of central Italy, in striking cities; their empire extended to Campania in the south and to the Po valley in the north (Figure 1). They traded across the Mediterranean. Their culture was full of art, music, technology, sport, wine, religion; they lived well and they knew it. Visitors to the region today are still seduced by the painted tombs at Tarquinia, the silent tumuli of Cerveteri (ancient Caere), the vertiginous hilltop sites such as Volterra. Museums are full of artworks of extraordinary skill and beauty, and Etruscan eyes stare at us from hundreds of sarcophagi, proudly defiant in the face of death and time.

Yet wherever one looks, in non-specialist guides, or in holiday brochures, one reads about the 'mysterious' Etruscans; hidden Etruria; underground Etruria—as if the culture is somehow concealed from us. It is a sales gimmick which has been very useful and profitable, but it is also misleading.

This *Very Short Introduction* starts from the premise that the Etruscans were no more mysterious than most other peoples of archaic Italy. Moreover, the tag of being mysterious has prevented the Etruscans from being properly integrated into narratives of classical history, and this is regrettable, because they offer a

1. Map of Italy showing Villanovan, Etruscan, and Greek settlements

fascinating counterpoint to the other more regularly discussed
Mediterranean cultures, including Rome and Athens. There is, in
fact, so much evidence that to do it justice requires a much bigger
book than this. In this account, the Etruscans are players in the
Mediterranean world, part of the manifold and multiple

2

connections and crossings of peoples, objects, and ideas over two millennia which make up the rich pattern of antiquity from the Bronze Age to the dwindling of the Roman empire in the west.

We begin with the two questions which have puzzled modern scholars, and have contributed to the claim that there is something peculiarly difficult about the Etruscans. Where did they come from and why is their language so odd? The first of these questions is neither unusual nor confined to the Etruscans; the Greeks spent a lot of time discussing their own origins but without much historical basis, and aficionados of Macedonian culture will be well aware of the endless controversy over whether it was Greek or not. The language issue is rather more unusual, but often misstated; we can read Etruscan, but it happens that most of what survives is not particularly informative.

Having addressed these two classic problems, the rest of the book is organized chronologically, from the later Bronze Age to the late Roman period; and concludes with an account of the way the Etruscans have been studied, and how that has contributed to their alleged 'mysteriousness'.

A major argument of this book is that a history of the Etruscans can be written; we have enough information to talk about social organization, aspects of political behaviour, economic behaviour at an urban and a regional level, cultural history, and so forth. That history has to be seen in the broader Mediterranean and Italian context, however, and one thread which runs through the book is how the Etruscans managed the connections they had to this wider world. Another intractable problem is what we mean when we talk about the Etruscans. Most of the individuals we discuss here are from a relatively privileged group. Discerning the poor in Etruria from the archaeological record is hard, and the poorest may not have been Etruscans but rather slaves. So this can only be a partial history, but it is important nonetheless to return what voice we can to the Etruscans and see beyond the museum artefacts.

Ancient Etruria was a region of Italy which ran from the Tiber north towards the Po, on the western side of the Apennine mountains. The coastal area is mostly plains, but inland are heavily dissected ranges of hills running both east–west and north–south. It is a landscape created by water, limestone, and distant volcanic activity, broken up but navigable; in parts agriculturally fertile, and in others rich in mineral resource (Figure 2). Today, it is divided into the modern administrative units of northern Lazio and Toscana, which map loosely onto the somewhat distinctive cultural groups of southern and northern Etruria. Then, as now and throughout its history, the region was characterized by independent cities controlling swathes of territory; the well-known hilltop settlements commanding their hinterland, and still showing traces of the vast Etruscan walls which surrounded them.

Etruria showed social development and sophistication in the Late Bronze Age (c.1300 to 900 BC). In the transition from the very end of the Bronze Age into the Iron Age (950–750 BC) the settlement patterns are radically transformed and it is clear that Etruria has undergone a revolution. Larger sites were created and territory came under different forms of control. In the 8th century, contemporary with the legendary foundation of Rome, the arrival of the Phoenicians and especially the Greeks from the east offered new opportunities and ideas, a new visual language for art, for religious expression, and for architectural display, and even a new alphabet. Etruscans were early and vigorous adopters, and 650 to 500 BC was a period of immense creativity and change. Conflicts inside and outside Etruria slowed the pace of change, brought social revolution in parts and the reduction of Etruscan territory. By 400 BC, the impact of the Romans was beginning to be felt; by 250 BC the Roman conquest was more or less complete, and the earliest Roman colonies were founded in Etruscan territory; by the mid-1st century, Etruscan autonomy was non-existent and the language increasingly rare, as land redistribution occasioned by Rome increasingly eroded the older

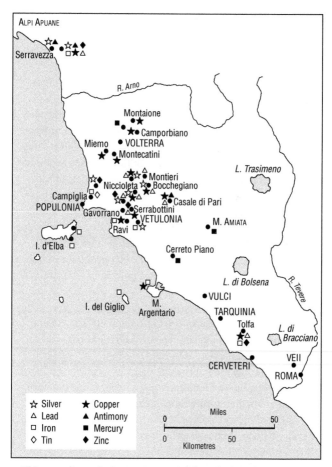

2. This map shows the intense concentration of mineral resources in the Etruscan region, especially around Populonia

cities' economic capacity. By the mid-1st century AD, Etruscan was scarcely spoken or understood, and the landscape had changed utterly, with large landowners and slave-based farming common. Somewhat unusually, I have chosen to give equal weight to Etruria after the Roman conquest, precisely because the way that most accounts ignore this period permits us to identify the Etruscans with their language, and justifies the idea that they disappear, leaving some mystery to resolve about what happened to them. Yet the period of transformation and the way the region accommodated the realities of Roman domination is as much a part of the history of the Etruscans and helped to form the Etruscan world the visitor sees today. There were large processes of economic and social transformation in later antiquity and it would not be until the early middle ages that the landscape would begin to be refilled with the new architecture of the emergent church and new forms of authority; by the Renaissance, Tuscany was once more one of the most powerful and distinctive regions in the world.

The Etruscans were always known to be different. 'They were a people with customs unlike anyone else,' said the Greek writer Dionysius of Halicarnassus, in the late 1st century BC, who had taken pains to study them. For some they were a warning of virtue abandoned; wealthy and indulgent, given to feasts and pleasure. Some focused on their piracy or on their cruelty. Their piety and religious knowledge were known, admired, feared, and ridiculed. It was an Etruscan soothsayer who warned Julius Caesar about the Ides of March. They were inventors; they were variously said to have invented the war trumpet, the triumph (which the Romans famously took over), boxing, gladiatorial games, the uniform and trappings of magistrates. The emperor Augustus' cultured friend Maecenas was proud to be descended from Etruscan kings.

Yet like almost all the peoples of the ancient world, they failed to hand on a literary tradition and history of their own. The Etruscan silence, compounded by the disappearance in antiquity of their own language, seems all the more deafening given the richness of their material culture, and their evident power for a good five centuries. The painstaking work of archaeologists and scholars however has gone a very long way to reviving knowledge of the Etruscans. The modern visitor to an Etruscan site or museum collection has absolutely no reason to feel bewildered or be left ignorant. Whilst there is much we will never know, there is much that we can say, and thrillingly, much more to discover.

Chapter 1

The origins of the Etruscans

There are two separate debates about the origins of the Etruscans, though they overlap and are hard to keep apart. One is about what the ancient sources thought, and why; and the other is about how we best explain change in the archaeological record, particularly in the context of the late Bronze and early Iron Age. The Etruscan case study deserves to be placed more firmly into debates about ancient ethnicity.

Ancient writers believed that there was something to be said about where peoples came from, and had a clear idea of ethnic identity. The Greeks saw themselves as different from others. Indeed the Greeks claimed that everyone who was not a Greek was a *barbaros* or barbarian, because their language sounded strange, although this included claims about other forms of uncivilized behaviour. However, the idea that ethnicity is in some sense an essential or primordial feature is, at least some of the time, disputable, and its use is, much of the time, disreputable. Ethnicity was constructed; it evolved, in part as a rhetorical strategy of self-identification.

The debate about Etruscan origins was prompted by the evidence of ancient literary sources. Herodotus, a Greek writer of the 5th century BC, describes how the Lydians were suffering from a very long famine. Things got so bad that drastic measures had to be taken:

Finally the king [Atys son of Manes] divided the people into two groups, and made them draw lots, one for staying and one for leaving the country; he would be king over those who drew the lot for staying, and his son, whose name was Tyrrhenus, would take the lot for those who were leaving. Those who had drawn the lot to leave the country, went down to Smyrna and built ships, and put on board everything that would be helpful for a sea voyage, and set off in search of livelihood and land, and after having stayed with many groups they came to the Ombrikoi, where they founded their cities and have lived until now. Instead of Lydians, they changed their name to that of the boy who had led them, and called themselves after him Tyrsenoi. (Herodotus 1.95).

By Herodotus' own reckoning, this must have taken place before the Trojan War, which is conventionally dated to the 12th century BC. He is followed by all sources who express an opinion except one, Dionysius of Halicarnassus, who wrote in the late 1st century BC. Dionysius makes two key points; first that the Etruscans were not the same as the so-called Pelasgians (contrary to a view apparently expressed in another passage in Herodotus) and second that there is every reason to believe that the Etruscans had always been in Italy, and no reason to believe that they were Lydians; their language, gods, and institutions have nothing in common.

We therefore have three theories: the Etruscans came from Lydia; the Etruscans were the same as the Pelasgians; or the Etruscans were native to Italy.

The Lydian theory was told to Herodotus by the Lydians themselves. What reliable information they may have had on the subject is unclear. The story looks like several Greek accounts of colonization in the aftermath of disaster and divine warning. This is a wholly artificial invention, and as such maybe served local functions we cannot now uncover. Once it had made its appearance in Herodotus, it was open to new interpretations, and every aspect of the Etruscans which seemed foreign could be seized on to prove the link.

The Pelasgian origin comes from a different tradition. The Pelasgians were thought to be the original settlers in Greece, and from that thought they become a sort of catch-all for the earliest settlers in the Aegean. There was no secure knowledge about them, or even their language. A number of Etruscan cities claimed descent from the Pelasgians, including Cerveteri and Tarquinia. The Greeks, and the Etruscans themselves, had to answer questions about the origins of Etruscan cities, and one way to do so was to integrate their history with that of the Greeks. So on this theory, the Etruscan cities were founded by migrant Pelasgians, which of course has the advantage that they were, in a sense, Greek. Alongside this, genealogical thinking could construct a mythical Tyrrhenos as the son of Telephos and grandson of Herakles; Cortona would claim the burial ground of Odysseus (known there as Nanas the wanderer). Thus Etruscan cities built up substantial prehistories in the same way as Greek cities had done; it is intriguing to see many images of Aeneas and his father Anchises, who escaped the sack of Troy by the Greeks, at Veii. Ultimately Rome would claim Aeneas, but there was competition over mythological founder figures.

The Pelasgian theory was complicated by an odd passage of Herodotus, who, in discussing the language of the Pelasgians, claims that it was still spoken in Creston 'beyond the country of the Tyrrhenians'. (Creston is otherwise known as a town in Thessaly, in northern Greece.) By the time the text had reached Dionysius of Halicarnassus, Creston had become Croton, and that was understood to be Cortona (not the town in Calabria which is also called Croton). The only thing that is clear is that there is a terrific muddle here. The language issue however was picked out, and became a key problem.

Etruscan is not an Indo-European language, and that is peculiar in Italy. It does look a bit like the language found on a stele (an inscribed marble stone) on the Greek island of Lemnos. So was there a genuine kinship? Unfortunately, the inscription can be interpreted in entirely different ways; it could represent a people in the east from whom the Etruscans are derived; a migration of Etruscans (few or many) eastwards; or an indication that there was from some great antiquity a group called Tyrrhenians both in the east and the west (which might then help explain how Herodotus manages to place them somewhere near Thessaly).

The opposite approach to a migration hypothesis is autochthony; the argument that a people had always been in a particular place. As we have seen, Dionysius of Halicarnassus chooses this theory. Autochthony is another way of explaining the oddness of the Etruscan language and religion; like the Egyptians, they are constructed as the other, not because they were outsiders but because they had been local for so long.

Inevitably, faced with these claims and counterclaims, modern scholars have wanted to find the answer, but all the scientific approaches were going nowhere, and in the aftermath of the Second World War, concentrating on dubious science to support claims of eastern or other origins was not a good way of advertising a discipline. Massimo Pallottino (1909–95), who might reasonably be described as the greatest Etruscologist of the 20th century, and had himself written a powerful book on the subject, called a halt; as he rightly pointed out, all the words that had been spilt had simply taken scholars around the disagreement between Herodotus and Dionysius of Halicarnassus, without advancing the situation. The really important question was what the Etruscans were actually like, not where they came from, formation rather than provenance. Studying the culture was the job of Etruscology.

This closed the argument for some time, and led to the major developments in scholarship which have characterized Etruscan studies over the past 50 years. Science however moves on, and recently the origin of the Etruscans has been back in the news, as efforts have been made to use DNA to establish the answer. One analysis of ancient bones suggested a great deal of continuity right back to the Neolithic period, which is close to the autochthonous argument. Another suggested human contacts with the east; and a third suggested that cattle had come from the east; and these were heralded as evidence that Herodotus was right. However, the date range on the human evidence was anywhere between 800 BC and AD 800, and cannot therefore be taken as conclusive proof of Herodotus' version of a migration generations before the 12th century Trojan War. What we may see from the evidence of maternal mitochondrial DNA is the movement of some women across the Mediterranean. In the context of the highly international elite which formed in the 8th century BC, this would be unsurprising.

So are the Etruscans still mysterious? There is no doubt that science will continue to advance, and over time we may arrive at a definitive answer to the question of where the Etruscans came from. If we do, it will be interesting, but one suspects that it will not sustain any of the historical accounts, all of which describe identities constructed in specific times and places and for highly contingent purposes. It is no criticism of Herodotus to say that the Lydians' story of their migrations probably has no basis in knowledge of what was even to them the distant past, and that even were the DNA to prove an eastern origin, it would not prove that the Lydians or Herodotus knew what they were talking about.

As for the question of origins, some at least might regard this as a matter of perspective. Looked at from a point of view that stretches back to the Palaeolithic, the expectation would be of movement over the *longue durée*. Everyone comes from somewhere, in other words. The debate remains unsettled over how revolutions in language and agriculture were spread in the Neolithic; was there an Indo-European people who flooded across Europe or were technological changes and habits spread by contact?

Whatever the answer to that, it would appear that there are corners of Europe which maintained their own languages; Basque is the standard example. The obstacle to this argument in the case of the Etruscans is that it is surprising that an area so rich and fertile was not the urgent object of some entrant people, since the rest of Italy spoke a language derived from Indo-European. If the Indo-European speaking peoples did indeed invade, why would they not have come to Tuscany?

Both in terms of archaeology and language there is some merit in looking north as well as east. As we shall see, in the later second millennium BC, there are strong parallels and connections with what is happening north and south of the Alps; and the one language in Italy which does seem a little like Etruscan is the poorly known Raetic. If there was a population movement, however, it can only be placed around 1200 BC or earlier; and if that is right then the Etruscans are not really any more mysterious than any of the other peoples of Italy. Nobody spends much time on questions about where the population of Rome in 1200 BC came from.

That takes us back to Pallottino's challenge. Aspects of Etruscan culture tempted the ancients to play a game of cultural association which they enjoyed. Ethnicity was an important concept in antiquity, and the Etruscan case study shows how many options could be developed. These, however, are questions about self-definition and external description—and they are more interesting ones to discuss than the question of where the Etruscans came from.

Chapter 2
The Etruscan language

Etruscan was not an Indo-European language; that is, it did not share the common inherited grammatical structures which most European languages have and which are usually thought to have spread in the Neolithic period along with farming techniques. That is what makes Etruscan difficult to understand. It is however perfectly possible to read Etruscan. From the 8th century on, the Etruscans used an alphabet which was derived from the Phoenicians and which was in use across the Mediterranean. The letter forms differ only slightly from those used by the Greeks at the same time, and although Etruscan maintains its alphabet so that by the 2nd century it looks very different from formal Greek alphabets, it is perfectly legible (Figure 3). (On the whole, Etruscan inscriptions are written right to left.)

This is the precise opposite of the decipherment of Linear B in Mycenaean Greece, where we did not understand the signs that were being used. When these were revealed to represent syllables we could see that the language was an early form of Greek, and the baked clay tablets were immediately more or less comprehensible. For Etruscan, we understand the alphabet but it spells out words we do not always recognize.

That said, we can make a decent stab at understanding most of what is written. Almost all Etruscan survives as inscriptions on

Phoenician		Archaic Greek					Latin
		Corinth	*Athens*	*Ionia*	*The West*		
𐤀 'Aleph		Α	Α	Δ	Α	Alpha	A
𐤁 Bet		ᒉ	B	B	B	Beta	B
𐤂 Girnel		Γ	Λ	Γ	⟨, C	Gamma	C, G
𐤃 Dalet		Δ	Δ	Δ	Δ, D	Delta	D
𐤄 He		B	E	E	E	Epsilon	E
𐤅 Vav		F	F	–	⌐, F	Digamma	F
𐤆 Zayin		I	I	I	I	Zeta	Z
𐤇 Ḥet		ᗺ	ᗺ	–	ᗺ	-h ⎫ (H) Eta	H
		–	–	ᗺ	–	ē ⎭	
𐤈 Ṭet		⊗	⊗	⊗	⊗	Theta	
𐤉 Yod		⋜	I	I	I	Iota	I
𐤊 Kaph		K	K	K	K	Kappa	K
𐤋 Lamed		↰	L	↰	L	Lambda	L
𐤌 Mem		Μ	Μ	Η	Μ	Mu	M
𐤍 Nun		N	Ν	N	N	Nu	N
𐤎 Samekh		Ξ	X	Ξ	⊞	Xi	X
𐤏 'Ayin		O	o	o	o	Omicron	O
𐤐 Pe		ᒋ	Γ	Γ	Γ	Pi	P
𐤑 Ṣade		Μ	–	–	Μ	San (= s)	
𐤒 Qoph		ϙ	(ϙ)	(ϙ)	ϙ	Koppa	Q
𐤓 Resh		Ρ	P	P	R	Rho	R
𐤔 Shin		–	⟨	⟨	⟨	Sigma	S
𐤕 Tav		Τ	Τ	Τ	Τ	Tau	T
		V	Υ	V	Υ	Upsilon	V, Y, U
		Φ	Φ	Φ	Φ	Phi	
		X	X	X	Ψ	Chi	
		✝	–	✝	–	Psi	
		–	–	Ω	–	Omega	

3. This chart shows the Phoenician, Greek, and Latin alphabets and illustrates their fundamental resemblance. The Etruscans used lightly modified versions of the Greek alphabet, written back to front, and with some local variations

stone or metal, or painted on pottery; and mostly as dedications, but there are some longer inscriptions, including three thin sheets of gold from Pyrgi (Figure 4), with a parallel Phoenician text, which relate the dedication of a temple or cult building. Two calendars of ritual also survive, one from Capua and the other the extraordinary linen book, 1,500 words long, which was torn up and used as the wrappings on a mummy, now to be found in Zagreb. But the vast majority of the words in Etruscan inscriptions are names. So, on a tomb at Volsinii, we read 'mi aranθia flavienas', which simply says 'I (am the tomb of) Aranth Flavienas'. There are about 12,000 inscriptions in all, and the majority are short and completely transparent.

The prevalence of names in the inscriptions has encouraged a careful study of Etruscan onomastic practice, and comparisons with other parts of Italy. Until the 8th century BC, individuals are attested with only one name. After the 8th century, and the substantial move towards more urbanized foundations, two names become common in much of central Italy. Instead of saying 'x, son of y' we find names constructed as 'x, of the family y' and so (technically) the patronymic adjective becomes a gentilicial nomen. Why was it important for the Etruscans and others at this point to make a clear reference to their extended family? It is widely assumed that this relates to transmission of property and that suggests something very significant about the structure of the family and the relationship between the family and more complex social structures. Moreover, nomenclature also reveals slaves, who have only a personal name and a reference to their owner; from Chiusi we find 'Antipater cicuσ' (Antipater—a Greek name—belonging to [i.e. slave of] Cicu).

4. (Opposite) Dated to around 500 BC, these three tablets, each about 10 cm by 20 cm, come from Pyrgi, the port site of Cerveteri. One is Phoenician-Punic, and is a dedication to Astarte; one in Etruscan is a dedication to Uni; the third mentions an annual festival. All three mention an Etruscan ruler called Thefarie Velianas

The Roman conquest placed pressure on Etruscan as a written language. There was no edict forbidding use of the language; rather the increasing influx of Latin-speaking settlers may have rendered the language less attractive, perhaps less comfortable to use; there is some evidence for Latin-speakers laughing at those who spoke either foreign languages or heavily accented Latin. At the same time, bilingualism was for a while an option.

We know of 28 Etruscan and Latin bilinguals, all from the late 2nd century BC into the 1st century AD, and they are not all elite. Lucius Scarpius, freedman of Scarpia and a priest's assistant from Perugia, is an intriguing example. The inscription was on an urn with a travertine marble cover, decorated with a gorgon's head on the body, and a rose and a bunch of grapes on the tympanum of the cover. The tomb included 15 urns and five funerary vessels; Scarpia's urn was nearby. The Etruscan version is misspelt; the person who freed Lucius was a woman—or was she his wife?

The most famous however is the funerary monument found at Pisaurum. In beautifully inscribed Latin and Etruscan letters, the inscription reads:

[L ·CA]FATIUS· L ·F ·STE· HARUSPE[X]
FULGURIATOR
(Translation: Lucius Cafatius, son of Lucius, of the voting tribe Stellatina, haruspex, interpreter of lightning strikes)

[c]afates· lr· lr ·netơ'vis· trutnvt ·frontac
(Translation: Laris Cafates, (son of) Laris, haruspex, interpreter of lightning strikes)

The inscription shows someone, perhaps the deceased or someone who commissioned the inscription, at ease with his ritual activity in both languages.

It is quite wrong therefore to say that we cannot read or understand Etruscan, but the inscriptions only get us so far. Certainly they could write at length—Etruscan books on ritual matters were consulted well outside Etruria, but alas none has survived.

Chapter 3
Towards the Etruscan city-state

Travellers who walked into an Etruscan settlement such as Veii or Cerveteri in the early 6th century BC would find themselves in a relatively familiar urban environment. Walls, gates, houses, roads, temples, water infrastructure would all be present. It would not feel very different from one of the contemporary Greek colonies of southern Italy, or from Athens and Corinth. The classic Mediterranean urban settlement—*polis* in Greece, *urbs* at Rome, and city-state used generically—is nevertheless not the only possible solution for aggregations of humans; it was the product of a series of choices over time.

Anyone studying Etruscan history must work with at least two rather different kinds of chronological schemata, neither of which uses the term 'Etruscan'. Where do these chronological classifications come from? Secure dating is rare, and on its own can only date an object not a context. So archaeologists work with sequences, usually derived from careful stratigraphic excavation, and typology, which depends on careful analysis of objects from individual sites and across whole regions, to get a sense of relative order. From that point, tools such as radiocarbon dating or dendrochronology can begin to help.

There is an understandable tendency to divide this relative order into periods. The old division into Stone, Bronze, and Iron Age was first developed in the 19th century and is still used today, though with increasingly fine differentiations and divisions. Often there is one key site which gives very good data for a particular phase. This then becomes the type site. In Etruria, one type site which has dominated the terminology is a cemetery with about 200 burials, mostly cremations, with the ashes in ceramic containers, from Villanova near Bologna, first found in 1853. This site was recognized to offer a kind of burial behaviour which could be found elsewhere across a large area of Italy, which was thereafter called Villanovan. In 1937, in order to differentiate a phase which was transitional to Villanovan and seemed chronologically earlier, the term proto-Villanovan was coined.

So an object from Veii in Etruria might be described as a Final Bronze Age proto-Villanovan object, or a Late Early Iron Age 1 Villanovan object belonging to Veii sequence 1B Toms (the last referring to the author of the standard classification and periodization at Veii, which superseded all previous efforts) dated to (give or take 25 years or so) 900 BC.

For the non-expert, this is bewildering and off-putting, so we will avoid this forest of terms, but in so doing one should not forget that the work that went into creating this level of accuracy was phenomenally difficult, and hugely valuable. But where does it leave the Etruscans? It is extremely important to note that there is no such people as the Villanovans. 'Villanovan' describes a pattern of cultural behaviour. Translating this into an ethnic identity makes as much sense as talking about the bowler hat people, or the iPod people. The question of Etruscan origins is lurking here again. In the 19th century, it was not clear whether the people buried in the cemetery at Villanova were the same as the people who would subsequently occupy Bologna in the 8th to 6th centuries, whom we are happy to call Etruscans. And what then about the relationship between proto-Villanovan culture and Villanovan culture? Recently, it has become clearer that there are real problems of perspective here. Proto-Villanovan and Villanovan culture in their broadest senses can be found over much of Italy, right down into Calabria, but the version of Veii and the version at Tarquinia 40 km away are subtly different. Furthermore if one does not believe in radical population migrations, but takes the view that the majority of the population from say 1200 to 600 BC were local to the area, what prevents us from calling them Etruscans all the way through?

One reason why this is important is that, at present, we identify the Etruscans only with their highly urbanized form, the city-state mentioned at the beginning, and this gives a degree of weight and teleological significance to that set of choices. Urbanization becomes the characteristic which defines the Etruscans; and if it is associated with the arrival of the Greeks, as it has been in the past, then we easily replace an account in which the Etruscans arrived from elsewhere with an account in which the model of culture which marks the Etruscans out from the possessors of Villanovan culture comes from elsewhere. If there is no strong ground to believe the population to have been changed radically by immigration, then there is an argument for seeing a series of developments in the use of landscape and resources, which relate to social and political changes, all taking place over a long period from the Recent Bronze Age to the 7th and 6th centuries BC.

Early Bronze Age settlements were largely on flat open sites; in northern Italy this culture is called Terramare culture and included substantial highly regular villages. Further south the settlements are more irregular and less organized. From the 13th century onwards, we see a shift in Etruria towards more defensible sites. Elsewhere in Italy, more dramatic changes can be seen—the complete disappearance of the Terramare culture in around 1200 BC for instance. It may therefore have been a period of some turbulence, and it is interesting that the preceding period has been identified as one in which greater social differentiation can be seen, and that in Etruria, in addition to the move to defensibility, we also see a greater emphasis on the production, use, consumption, and deposition of bronze. Social hierarchy requires a material underpinning, and bronze may have become increasingly important, but social hierarchy is also fragile. Certainly we know that before 1200, some Mycenaean pottery can be found in Italy, indicating trade links with the eastern Aegean. In the 12th century, much of the infrastructure of the eastern Mediterranean collapsed.

Sovana is an example of one of these settlements at the beginnings of this new phase. Although the site, not far from the Lago di Bolsena, shows signs of activity from much earlier in the Bronze Age, it is only in the Final Bronze Age that we find signs of a permanent settlement. The settlement is interrupted around 900 to be later reoccupied under the influence of Vulci in the 6th century. Not far away, Sorgenti della Nova shows a similar pattern of occupation. Covering perhaps 15 hectares and with a population around 1,500 at a maximum, the site has produced evidence of animal husbandry as well as crops. There were various house forms, including one very substantial house, rock-cut grottos, possible cult activity, and pottery kilns. Luni sul Mignone, near Blera, is slightly different in that it shows a rather clearer and more substantial earlier phase from at least the middle of the second millennium, but then shows the same focus on the defensible area of the site, and abandonment in the early first millennium. Finally, San Giovenale, again not far from Blera, shows much stronger signs of continuity from an equally early phase across into the Iron Age and the Etruscan period.

The variability of the settlement pattern is coupled with an increasingly differentiated material culture. It was a slow process, but the larger question is the extent to which it was a collective process. This is one of the hardest questions to answer because the material culture is still insufficiently distinct to permit one to see one site influencing another, but there are signs of imports and trade movements, especially from the north and the area of the Danube. A key site which connects the areas is Frattesina. Larger than many contemporary sites in the Po Valley it shows substantial productive activity in ceramics, amber, and glass. Ivory and an ostrich egg show trade with the middle east or north Africa. Frattesina is hugely important as a link between the late Bronze Age and the Iron Age, and it gives a hint as to the international opportunities and the potential markets and economic interactions which underpinned the transformation in Early Iron Age Etruria.

Chapter 4
The Villanovan revolution

The Villanovan revolution can now be seen as a complex development, with roots back in the Late Bronze Age; and it can also be seen to have clear comparisons across a substantial amount of Italy, in the Po Valley, Emilia Romagna, Tuscany, Lazio, and Campania. Some new sites were created, others have traces of earlier occupation. The sites chosen are large, strategically located, extensively utilized, with necropoleis outside the settlements. There is a jump from settlements with a few tens of individuals to sites with some hundreds of people; but, correspondingly, there are fewer settlements further from each other. One can compare the cluster of sites around the Lago di Bracciano for instance with the more dispersed map of the large centres.

One of the best-known examples is Veii, a few kilometres across the river Tiber from Rome. The large plateau is occupied from the early Iron Age, with evidence of settlement at a number of discrete sites. Distinct burial sites, and settlement are scattered across an area in the region of about 175 hectares. At Tarquinia and Cerveteri, evidence is growing for late Bronze Age settlement before a major increase in the early Iron Age. The great Etruscan cities of the 7th and 6th centuries all have their roots in this transformation (Figure 5).

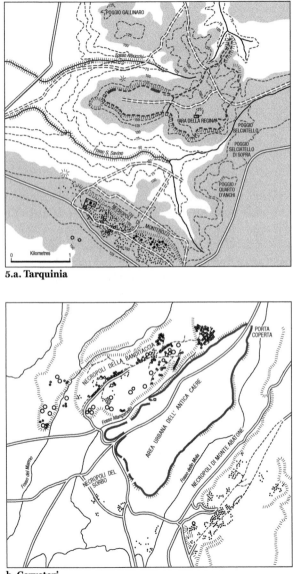

5.a. Tarquinia

b. Cerveteri

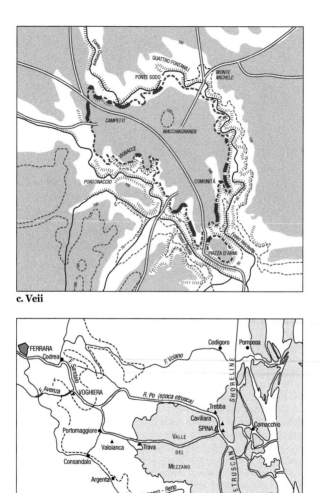

c. Veii

Labels in map c:
Fosso Cannetaccio
QUATTRO FONTANILI
MONTE MICHELE
PONTE SODO
CAMPETTI
MACCHIAGRANDE
VIGNACCE
PORTONACCIO
COMUNITÁ
Fosso Piordo
Fosso Valchetta
PIAZZA D'ARMI

d. Spina

Labels in map d:
FERRARA
Codrea
Codigoro
Pomposa
F. Volano
SHORELINE
Sandalo
F. Avenza
VOGHIERA
R. Po (epoca etrusca)
Trebba
Caviliara
SPINA
Comacchio
Portomaggiore
VALLE
Valoianca
Trava
DEL
MEZZANO
ETRUSCAN
Consandalo
Argenta
R. Po di Primaro - Reno

0   Kilometres   10

27

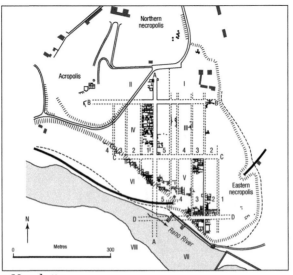

e. Marzabotto

5. a. Around 120 hectares in size, the city began on the Piano della
    Civita, and the walls were extended in the 4th century to include
    the neighbouring plateau which was dominated by the large temple
    known as Ara della Regina. The Necropolis di Monterozzi can be
    seen over a kilometre away

    b. Covering over 150 hectares, the plateau was fully occupied from
    the 6th century. Ravines separate the urban plateau from the
    neighbouring plateaux which were used for burials. The Necropolis
    della Banditaccia contains some of the oldest and largest of the
    chamber tombs, as well as later and more regularly aligned tombs

    c. About 20 km northwest of Rome, Veii covered a broad plateau,
    and appears to be a particularly clear example of how distinct
    settlements with different burial grounds gradually in the 9th
    century grew closer together and by the end of the 7th century had
    developed a clear sense of community. The major temple at Piazza
    d'Armi is early; the Portonaccio temple produced magnificent
    terracotta statuary which survived because it was broken up and
    buried after the Roman victory. The site never really recovered,
    but in the Roman period had a bath building and villa complex

Scattered evidence in the countryside shows that the landscape was not deserted, and the pace of change varies somewhat from site to site, but there is less early Iron Age material distributed across Etruria than there is in the later Bronze Age or the subsequent period. So what caused this concentration of settlement?

One clue may lie in the evidence for increased rural settlement towards the end of the Bronze Age; the rise in population and settlement may have permitted and/or encouraged concentration. Certainly, the major centres required substantial populations, but whilst this may be a contributory factor, it cannot by itself explain the Villanovan revolution. We have to consider two characteristic and related forms of evidence, burials, and settlement.

Burials, in ditches, or other cavities, covered and protected, resist destruction better than huts and houses of wattle and daub. Burial evidence is therefore fundamental to our ability to understand ancient societies, but it is not methodologically straightforward. The ways in which one may wish to represent an individual or a group at the point of deposition in a funerary context is not necessarily an accurate representation of their situation in life.

As a consequence, we need to be alert to the challenges of understanding a living society from the way it treats its dead. For example, it is clear that we seldom have the evidence of all the deceased who can have lived in a community. Formal burial in a specified location may have been confined to a small proportion of society. So we may only ever see a fraction of a society, probably the elite; and it is also clear that very young children

d. The map shows how significant water was to Spina—by the sea and along the ancient course of the Po, it was perfectly positioned to take advantage of trade by sea and river
e. The map shows the regular grid plan of this unusual Etruscan settlement, founded in the 6th century in the Po Valley

are under-represented in necropoleis. Occasional evidence of the burial of babies inside houses may indicate that before a certain age, children were exempt from the rule of burial outside the city, which may imply that they had not attained a sufficient identity or personhood to be accorded that privilege. These sorts of approaches to the study of the ritual of burial do have a helpful consequence, though, for if burial was indeed managed and manipulated, then we can assume intentionality behind what we see. In other words, we may not be entitled to assume that the way a person or group is represented in death is precisely the same as the way s/he/they were seen in life, but we may be justified in believing that this representation does reflect the way a society wished that individual or group to be understood. Burial is often a demonstration to others, and it has sufficient potential for social disruption to be subject to rules and prohibitions.

Basic roles seem to be reflected in grave goods. Most burials in the 12th to the 9th century BC were cremations. The ashes of the deceased were placed in a container and buried, together with other goods, both ceramic and metal. Cremation subsequently and widely gives way to inhumation. One can analyse buried remains for gender and we tend to find that what one might think of as typically male goods such as weaponry or female goods such as spindle whorls, used in spinning wool, do usually follow the expected gender lines.

One may assume therefore that at the point of burial, a selection of goods was made which to a degree reflected aspects of the social persona of the deceased; the role they had in society, and the functions they fulfilled. To some extent, these are also age dependent. Warfare is the province of healthy adults, not children or old men, but an old man may retain the weapons he used when young. Older women sometimes accumulated more ceramic vessels than younger ones, and that might indicate a greater degree of control over the household. It is important not to underplay the significance of this; if we are right to see cooking and spinning as largely the responsibility of women, then they were also responsible for crucial economic activities, and may have wielded significant authority.

If we look at the earliest tombs in the Grotta Gramiccia, Casale del Fosso, and Quattro Fontanili cemeteries at Veii, we can see more precisely how the picture has been built up. Grotta Gramiccia was excavated between 1913 and 1918; Casale del Fosso in 1915–16, and Quattro Fontanili in the 1960s and 1970s. The necropoleis are generally similar but with slight variations. Individual male and female burials often seem connected—sometimes collocated. In the 8th century, the areas in between attract more burials, so it has been assumed that we can see the beginnings of a lineage group. Cremation and inhumation are both found, with inhumation becoming more common over time. The early cremations tend to use urns, sometimes inside other containers, often with some sort of cover. The accoutrements of war include helmets, swords, lances, axes, and shields, sometimes in miniature versions, predominantly made of iron. These do not appear, on the whole, with what are thought to be female accoutrements; pins, spindle whorls, and bobbins. The outcome overall is a picture of a society dominated by familial connections, which preserved and valued gender-differentiated roles. Within the overall community of Veii, difference and distinction existed in the context of a largely uniform culture (and one could say the same about Veii in the broader context—it is similar to, but not identical with, other Villanovan sites). Warfare and perhaps the hunt were clearly significant markers of status, but economic activity was also important, and the community could command—and afford to put out of use in burial—ceramics and metalwork.

Much ingenuity was expended on the containers for the deceased across Etruria. Some used a helmet as a cover for the pot. In some cases, the container was a model of a hut, and this evidence can be put together with evidence from post holes to give an idea of what a Villanovan settlement might have looked like. The huts were simple enough; a series of posts in an oval or roughly rectangular

6. This hut urn, from Cerveteri in the 6th century, shows both the enduring nature of this form of cinerary container, but also the evolution of domestic architecture; this is similar to the more regular stone built architecture of the 6th century

form were infilled with wattle and daub, and surmounted by a roof of reeds. They vary from about 5 m by 3.5 m to about 12 m by 6 m. Some of the hut urns used to contain ashes show a high degree of decoration; the same decoration may have been painted onto the walls of these huts, and is seen on pottery and on the few surviving scraps of textiles (Figure 6). One can imagine a highly developed but also consistent iconography.

There are several sites where we can see the traces of huts—one of the most substantial is at Tarquinia, where we can see 25 huts in the Monterozzi district, in an area of about 200 m by 100 m. Their shape—oval, rectangular, and square—might reflect functional distinctions, but on the whole the assumption has tended to be that huts are multi-functional. So what sort of society was it?

The tendency has been to think of Villanovan society as to some degree egalitarian. It is indeed hard to spot very clear differentiations between the individuals we see. Most of the goods found in tombs within any site are more or less at the same level between comparable individuals. There are few instances of very wealthy tombs and very poor ones in the same necropolis. Huts might differ in size or shape, but within limited parameters. One might imagine that most of the family groups who are represented were on a par with each other. Of course, that does leave a question as to whether everyone in Villanovan society was equal, and arguably, what we are seeing is a group of leaders who chose a more or less egalitarian ideology, within an archaeologically invisible wider society. Moreover, we should not discount the non-material indices of wealth, for instance the number of mourners at the burial, the lavishness of feasting, the amount of material available but not buried, and then subsequently reused, if it was metalwork.

The critical issue to which one returns is that the Villanovan revolution is a territorial one. Smaller distributed settlements were gathered into larger conglomerations, leaving the countryside, in some instances, somewhat empty for a century or more; over 90 per cent of late Bronze Age sites are abandoned. This is a clear, conscious, and political act. Most of the Villanovan centres are on larger plateaux, and have defensive capacity, but their size is so large that they also have the capacity for storage inside the site. Often strategically positioned, they all exceeded the previous settlements, either on those sites or elsewhere. This major shift led to economic and demographic growth; within three generations, the sites were filling up, necropoleis were diversifying, territory was being reoccupied.

It is easy to argue that the consequences of an act were connected to its causes, that these eventually economically successful settlements were created in the pursuit of economic success. There are good reasons for being cautious about inferring such a high degree of collective foresight. Yet there is no doubt that in every case, the major settlements had a clear control of known resource, albeit with variations. Veii, Cerveteri, Tarquinia, and Vulci all dominate fertile agricultural areas, and have access to the sea. Populonia and Vetulonia are oriented towards the mineral riches of Elba, with connections also to Sardinia. Of the slightly smaller sites, Bisenzio and Orvieto/Volsinii may give a clue as to unsuccessful transformation; too close to each other perhaps, Bisenzio, with slightly idiosyncratic burial practices, faded away in the 6th century. Chiusi and Vulci had control over local trade routes but flourished eventually in part through their artistic capacity.

The capacity to exploit, control, and store the product of the resources available was greater with larger sites. The move towards greater defensiveness may reflect some degree of resource warfare—after all, all those weapons in burials, unless they were solely for show or for intranecine strife, must have had a function. The processes of opportunity and competition encouraged concentration and this in turn required new ways of ordering socio-political relations.

As an example of the degree of potential strain this may have placed on societies, and the extreme ways in which they may have responded, at Tarquinia, we may now see a sequence of ritual acts at the Civita plateau. A hut was marked out, and it has been suggested that in the late 9th century, a child who was (according to the scientific analysis of the remains) albino, encephalopathic, and epileptic was buried there, perhaps as an expiatory act? Fifty years or so later, we see what may have been the sacrifice of an adult male. Infant burials then preceded each new building, in which unusual burials continued. Whether or not this remarkable interpretation is correct, this is an aspect of Villanovan society which is not easy to discern—the control of ritual power. However, we may guess that some of the senior figures within the settlements derived their authority in some way from a combination of raw force and charisma. The cult of ancestors, and the concentration on specific relationships between settlement and necropolis, may have been at the heart of the construction of authority, and that takes us back to the huts. The construction of buildings which served only a religious function is a development of the 6th century. Up until then, huts seem to have had multiple functions and one might suppose that one of them was related to the maintenance of a relationship with a spiritual world.

The Villanovan revolution was a transformation of the use of resource; an intensification which may have had its roots in the steady development of the later Bronze Age, but which radically reordered social relations. Recent debates over the absolute chronology of this shift have suggested that the early Iron Age may have been rather longer than we thought before. The closer chronological relationship with developments in northern Italy and central Europe may be pointing us to ways in which to understand the impetus behind the changes we see early in the Iron Age.

In the 13th and 12th centuries BC, the substantial civilizations of Mycenaean Greece and the east in general had begun to stretch westwards, and we can see Mycenaean pottery both in southern Italy and as far north as Frattesina. In the 12th and 11th centuries, a complex phenomenon of collapse in the east led to the destruction of the Mycenaean palaces and a phase of retrenchment and relative decline. Instability and insecurity across the Mediterranean must have affected parts of Italy too as the eastern contacts dried up. But Etruria in particular had access to another world. As central Europe developed, the demand for metal and the capacity for exchange grew. This may not have been a straightforward process but it may explain why in the Po valley and further south, perhaps as a delayed reaction to disruptions elsewhere, perhaps as an opportunistic choice, and probably as a combination, a culture developed which favoured larger sites, stronger communities, with powerful leadership developing over time. The consequences of these changes would be seen in the 8th century.

Chapter 5

The transformation
of Etruria

Verucchio, near Rimini on the Adriatic coast of Italy, represents
an interesting example of the potential of Villanovan society. The
necropolis and settlement ran from the 9th to the 6th centuries
BC. The site itself is about 300 m high and 17 km from the coast.
It is characterized by unusually wealthy late 8th century grave
goods, which include a splendid throne, with scenes of weaving
and procession, which may mark out an individual with a
combination of roles in war and priesthood. The grave goods
include gold and stunning amber pieces, demonstrating a close
link with the Danubian trade routes from which amber was
largely derived. Verucchio seems largely indigenous. Like the
major centre in northern Etruria, Bologna, these sites look
northwards and across the Adriatic, and trade and communicate
with each other directly. It is also notable that, unlike southern
Etruscan settlements such as Cerveteri and Tarquinia, Verucchio
faded away in the 6th century.

When one enters the great Etruscan museum collections, such as
the Archaeological Museums of Florence or Bologna, or the Villa
Giulia in Rome, one is struck by how much Greek pottery there is.
The majority of surviving intact pottery which was made in the
Greek cities of Corinth and Athens was discovered in the tombs of
Etruria. Josiah Wedgwood, when he named the factory which
created his classically inspired ceramics, called it Etruria. Students

of Greek ceramics have to acknowledge the fact that for the most part they are describing an export market; when Italian museums rejoice at the return of items illicitly taken from Etruscan sites, the objects are often Greek pots.

The Greeks came in numbers to live in southern Italy and Sicily, in settlements we call colonies, and the Greeks called *apoikiai*, 'homes away', from the mid-8th century BC. For about 200 years there was a vigorous and then diminishing process of settlement. These colonies traded and exchanged with central Italy (the most northerly colony was Cumae). Greeks from mainland Greece traded with their colonies too, and fell out with them. The main visible trace element of this trade is pottery, used for cups and plates and so forth (open vessels) and also amphorae, perfume containers, and other forms (closed vessels) which carried goods which were also therefore being traded, including wine (Figure 7). From 650 or so until about 550 BC, the majority of the pottery came from Corinth, and thereafter the majority came from Athens, though that is not to say that the individuals carrying the pottery were necessarily Corinthians or Athenians; these were the fashionable labels of their day.

Over time, we can see Etruscan cities creating temples that look somewhat like Greek temples (they have columns and the cult statue is inside and under a roof, although they are in other ways distinctive), statues which imitate Greek examples, naming and picturing deities who are either completely taken over from the Greek world (Aplu/Apollo) or have begun to look Greek (Uni is a bit like Hera but she is also like other deities). So it was not difficult for scholars to assume that the Greek influence was inescapable in all areas. Now, however, the debate has become even more interesting.

It has been known for some time that the westward push of the Greeks was strongly influenced by events and processes further east. The Assyrian empires of Mesopotamia were hugely

7. 36.3 cm high, this crater from a tomb in Cerveteri shows on one side a naval battle perhaps between Greeks and Etruscan pirates, and on the other the Homeric scene of the blinding of Polyphemus. Dated to around 650 BC, it is inscribed in Greek with the words 'Aristonothos made me'. So this would appear to be produced by a Greek immigrant to Cerveteri, who had maintained some of his local knowledge, but had also adapted to more local traditions

dependent on external sources of goods which were then used to lubricate the social and political structures that supported the great kings. Along the coastal littoral of current Lebanon and Syria, the Phoenicians proved able mediators; plying their crafts back and forth across the Mediterranean, they encouraged trade, and their settlements, often situated on the edges of countries or on offshore islands, comprised mixed and intermarrying populations who were motivated by exchange and not by the desire to settle. Only at Carthage (and Gades) did the Phoenicians build a major city.

In the 10th century the Phoenicians were certainly present in Cyprus and perhaps further afield. For the Greeks, emerging from the problems attendant on the collapse of Mycenaean palace society, their arrival appears to have been galvanizing; and by around 775 BC, Greeks had joined Phoenicians in the first Italian venture, at Pithecusae. Phoenician influence would extend all the way to the straits of Gibraltar; the Greeks however had found a different approach, and increasingly came to stay in Italy. The colony of Cumae demonstrates this well; whilst Pithecusae is a small island off the coast, a classic Phoenician settlement, Cumae, founded on the opposite mainland a generation after Pithecusae, displaced a local population.

A by-product of this Phoenician–Greek interplay was the high visibility of eastern imagery. From eastern materials such as ivory, to lions and monsters on pottery, to Egyptian scarabs, to ostrich eggs, to Cypro-Phoenician gilt silver bowls; the rage for things eastern is so pervasive that it resembles the mid-18th century obsession with Chinoiserie. But this trend, which has traditionally been called orientalizing, is a complex blend of artistic taste and strong political messages about the adoption of an iconology of power, that is, a collection of images which refer to the huge power and wealth of the east and which, by being adopted into the Italian context, in some sense borrows some of that eastern power.

The Etruscan response to this wave of population movement is especially interesting. There are no Greek colonies so far north, yet orientalizing objects are rapidly found in and imitated at Etruscan sites. By the later 8th century we find imports of Euboean pottery, and by the 7th century, the Etruscan adoption of a range of artistic motifs and cultural behaviours from the Greeks and further east takes off. This accompanied an upsurge in display, wealth, and elite behaviours. The isomorphic tendencies of Villanovan society are left behind; Etruria becomes a land of highly competitive and highly visible aristocrats.

This is the period when scholars start talking about the Etruscans. As we have argued, this is rather false; there is no evidence of any population movement, no evidence of any upheaval which would mark a rupture with the preceding Villanovan culture. The Etruscans did not emerge in the 8th century—they had been around for at least two centuries although one might argue that their culture became more defined in this period. The next question is a chronological one; did the Etruscans develop their culture because of the arrival of the Greeks? In my view, the answer to this is no twice over; no, because the Phoenicians are critical to the argument; and no, because the Etruscans had already developed many of the characteristic features of their political and social organization.

One of the most interesting finds on Pithecusae, the island opposite the coast of Campania where Phoenicians and Greeks first settled, is a piece of slag from iron, which chemical analysis shows came from Elba, opposite the Etruscan city of Populonia. In other words, the Phoenicio-Greek settlement was importing raw material from Etruria. However important culturally the Greeks might become, it was the drive for resource which forged a link between Etruria and the east. Populonia sees a major increase in population density in the second half of the 9th century BC—before any Greek settlement known to us. The Phoenicians and Greeks entered a world where the Etruscans had already made a significant social, economic, and political step forward. The larger Etruscan settlements were in a good position to profit from the arrival of their eastern neighbours. This is not just a banal debate over priority. It would be absurd to deny the significance of the eastern influence on Etruria. Comparing the huge advances which southern Etruria makes, being closer and more accessible to the Greek colonies, and the rather different fate of Verucchio further north, is not entirely fair, but there is no doubt that the Greek world made a huge difference to the lifestyle, resources, culture, and ambition of the southern Etruscan cities in particular.

The Mediterranean was characterized in antiquity by an astonishing density of interactions and networks. Exchange of goods and ideas was fast and exponential. The Phoenicians were certainly closely engaged with the Euboeans late in the 9th century; just a few decades later, letters of their alphabet were already being used in local contexts in central Italy.

It was also a world of significant mobility. Greek colonization is one manifestation of this. Mobility within Italy, and between aristocratic families, and from west to east can also be traced. The Etruscans did not passively receive the cultures of the east; the engagement with orientalizing culture came at the end of a long period of steady growth in population, in settlement size and complexity, in complexity of ritual behaviour and artistic representation. Once we remove the boundary between Villanovan culture and the Etruscans, and recognize that the same people were driving forward economically and politically for 200 years before the arrival of the Phoenicians and the Greeks at Pithecusae, and once we give full credit for the complexity and interest of that process, the idea that the Etruscan barbarians absorbed Greek or any other culture unthinkingly looks implausible.

The Etruscans and the sea

Movement and exchange are constants in antiquity. It is a feature of the rupture after the collapse of Mycenaean palace society in Greece that we seem to see less movement, although there are still indications of continuities of exchange, at least at a relatively local level. The Mediterranean can be seen in terms of a map of interactions and networks, some on a very local scale, but fitting into much wider movements. Ship technology was advanced, and during the sailing season, we must imagine a world turned towards the sea, for food, for resources, and for information.

The major Etruscan cities which emerged from the Villanovan revolution were no exception. Cerveteri, Tarquinia, Vulci, Roselle, Vetulonia, and Populonia were all just inland, and Veii and Volterra were connected to the sea by the Tiber and the Cecina rivers respectively. Both Cerveteri and Tarquinia had port sites within their territory—Pyrgi and Gravisca. Even before the arrival of the Phoenicians and the Greeks, the Etruscans were clearly engaged in exchange, and the island of Sardinia is a critical part of this story. Similarly, we find unusual and highly specific forms of production, and intriguing relationships with Cyprus to the east (dating as far back as the 13th century) and Spain to the west.

Increasingly one sees mixtures of material from different places, implying a complex interconnected trading pattern. Etruria was involved in the later 9th and early 8th century, and what brought the Etruscans into the exchange cycle was precisely the combination of social and economic development and raw resources, especially mineral resources, which would make Etruria so interesting to the Phoenicians and Greeks.

The arrival of new ideas and possibilities from the east soon attracted movement in the opposite direction. Very early in this cycle, high concentrations of Euboean pottery have been found at Al Mina in the Levant. Later in the 8th century, Etruscan goods are found in Greek sanctuaries, and the tradition continues; one Arimnestos has the honour of being the first Etruscan king (according to the Greek writer Pausanias) to dedicate a throne in bronze to Zeus at Olympia, and it was still visible in his day (2nd century AD). But exchange could take many forms.

'Are you a pirate?' was a common, and not necessarily insulting, way to start a conversation with a stranger. Both the Phoenicians and the Etruscans were often called pirates in the sources. Exchange operated on many different levels; from theft to gift. Herodotus tells us of silent trade, where items were placed on a beach by one party, who then withdraw; others came, chose what they wanted, and left other goods in exchange, and then they withdrew. When things went wrong, being inland no doubt helped, and maybe this is why Cerveteri and Tarquinia were located where they were. We know nothing of Etruscan views of trade, but towards the end of the 7th century, the commercial expansion of the Etruscans took off. For the most part, Cerveteri and Vulci were the leaders, and they were shipping impasto, bucchero (a characteristic Etruscan near-black pottery), and Etrusco-Corinthian pottery to southern France, Spain, Corsica, Sardinia, Carthage, Sicily, and Campania. Some of these vessels are containers for wine, oil, and perfume. These Etruscans were imitating not only the material culture of the Greeks, but also their trading behaviour, and no doubt benefiting in return. By the 6th century, the western Mediterranean was a contested area with several powers competing with each other to hold supremacy amid fluid boundaries of influence and control.

The emergence of elites

Funerary goods show the clearest early evidence of the emergence of powerful elites who were prepared to flaunt their wealth in the most conspicuous way—by removing it from use. The new forms of goods which became available to the elite as a result of foreign trade and exchange enhanced the capacity to compete conspicuously. Moreover we have to remember that in burial we see only a part of the behaviour of this elite, and must guess at the rest (Figure 8).

Display and competition were at the heart of many of the dynamics we see in antiquity. Both at the level of individuals and of communities, we find strong tendencies towards rivalry, and these underpin behaviour which drove further developments. As far as we can tell, a great deal of early warfare in the Mediterranean is highly ritualized boundary drawing. It was a dangerous competition, and in time would escalate disastrously, but it was also a way of constructing community internally by creating external foes against whom unity was necessary. Sport was another mechanism, and the Etruscans were believed to have invented boxing and gladiatorial games, whilst the Greeks conducted their festival games, such as the Olympic Games. All this boundary testing, training, and management of energy in

8. A two-chamber tomb from around 510 BC, Tarquinia. The first chamber has paintings of the return from the hunt, a grove, and banquet scenes . The second chamber has a banquet scene in the pediment, and below it a seascape showing birds, fishes, and a diver. Variously interpreted, the tomb seems to show an idealized version of life either in this world, or in the next

increasingly community-oriented directions may be part of the complicated business of bringing together groups which had a dangerous tendency to fission.

Villanovan settlements were small communities, which drew population from the surrounding territory and were formed of discrete areas, which may have had a basis in extended descent groups. How could these groups be persuaded to collaborate and cooperate? How did they harness the energy and drive necessary to survive in a landscape which also contained competitors, without permitting it to become internally harmful? It was a complex balance.

One classic example of this balance is the concept of the gift. Gifts could also set up inequalities; a gift that cannot be matched brings shame and disgrace on the unfortunate recipient. Competition could destroy the wealth of individuals who engaged in unwise efforts to exceed others in generosity.

The appearance of increasingly wealthy goods in burial contexts in the 8th century, and indeed the construction of increasingly visible tombs in some instances, notably the chamber tombs with their corridors inside great mounds, leading to chambers with multiple burials, are aspects of this competition and its socialization within community. Tombs with very similar and highly luxurious contents are the Tomba Regolini-Galassi in Cerveteri and the Tomba Bernardini and the Tomba Barberini found at Praeneste (modern Palestrina) in Latium. It looks as if the occupants were connected, perhaps by marriage.

Warrior equipment does not appear in female burials, but both men and women are found in burials with chariots, some but not all of which were probably designed for the battlefield. Both men and women are shown participating in the community, and supporting its activities, whether that be in productive economic activity (weaving); feasting and banqueting (social competition); or warrior activity (communal competition and defence). This amalgam of activity is defining a household at a high level, capable of comfort, orderliness, and valour. Knives may reflect sacrificial activity. Chariots are expensive themselves, and they are also associated with horses (which are sometimes buried with the chariot, presumably having been sacrificed at the grave). Horses in antiquity are indicators of prestige; expensive to maintain, and largely used to ferry the elite in a very conspicuous way to the battlefield. Fighting was still on foot.

The chariot burials are also interesting because they are so widespread in Italy—one can find them in Latium, Campania, the Faliscan region, and Picenum. Moreover, whilst they are associated on the one hand with personal ornaments for women such as silver, gold, amber, and glass paste, they are also associated with drinking and feasting accoutrements, vessels and fire dogs, in both male and female contexts. In other words, both men and women were part of the world of what one might, loosely, call heroic display.

Heroic households

By the time of the arrival of the Greeks, the Etruscans were already participating in a competitive society in which values of strength and personal charisma were becoming recognized and having to be managed. In the Aegean world, precisely the same general characteristics can be identified. When the Greeks emerged from the traumatic aftermath of the fall of the Mycenaean palaces they remembered the stories of those days. The oral traditions preserved stories about the Trojan War, and about the gods, goddesses, and heroes who had participated in them. Some of the details had been preserved from the earliest times, fossilized in the verses which were sung and repeated.

Whether or not some individual called Homer ever existed to give such a focus to the poems is for us less relevant than the clear evidence that these stories, and others in the mythical cycles, were well known, and that they were a repository of values and ideas from which the Greeks drew almost constant inspiration. Scenes from the stories which are included in the *Iliad* and *Odyssey* appear early in decorative pottery exported from Greece to Etruria; Odysseus blinding the monstrous Cyclops Polyphemus on the Aristonothos vase (now in the Capitoline Museum in Rome) is an important example.

The Homeric stories taught Greeks many things. Men who listened to songs about heroes, and identified with them, knew that the gods were not far away. The stories also reinforced but sometimes problematized social distinctions; at the least, there are various versions of what it is to be a good leader. It is often said that Homer was the Greek Bible, but it was not only the Greek Bible. Homer and all the other non-Trojan War myths (Seven against Thebes, the archetypal fratricidal conflict, Jason and the Argonauts and the fascinating but scary Medea, Perseus slaying Medusa, Herakles and his exploits) were quintessentially Greek, but they had a broad appeal because they were wonderful stories and they could be depicted at least in shorthand on painted pottery. So the stories travelled with the Greeks, and then became part of a wider culture.

There is much more that could be said here. The language of mythology cannot be dissociated from the imaginative and emotional content of lived religion, and yet is also a mechanism of understanding and responding to the world. Mythological narratives instantiated ideas of beauty and virtue, but they also embodied concepts of danger and the precariousness of life.

Did everyone in Etruria know how to read a Greek pot with a Homeric myth on it? Did they take the same messages from Homeric stories as Greeks did? Did they feel themselves to be outsiders or insiders to a Greek world? Much of this is now beyond answer, but we can get hints. One of the most remarkable is an early 7th century bucchero pesante jug with a representation of Jason and Medea—their names are transcribed into Etruscan. Already then this myth could be seen as capable of being naturalized. Did the Etruscans think of themselves as the mysterious distant other represented by Medea, or did the Greeks seem to have that aura? That perhaps is unclear, but that

Etruscans could apply some of the values derived from the Greek stories to their own experience is indubitable.

This excursus is directly relevant to the progress of the Etruscan elite. It used to be thought that the Greeks brought viticulture to Italy, but we now know that the vine was cultivated before their arrival. However, the Etruscans did learn from the Greeks some of the techniques of the banquet, and they certainly poured wine from Greek jugs, drank from Greek cups, and ate from Greek plates. The ideology of the feast is central to Etruscan life and may carry through into death. The imagery of the banquet is often found on the walls of Etruscan tombs.

The combination of a developing Etruscan elite, the evolving iconography of heroism, and the actual accoutrements of the vast wealth from the east was a heady cocktail. We see the transformation largely in grave goods, and the introduction of Corinthian pottery. Corinthian pottery is less direct in its evocation of the Greek myths than later Attic ware, but the phenomenon we are tracing is the adoption of an orientalizing lifestyle, one might say, or of a lifestyle which is characterized by the internalization of ideas, representations, thoughts that belong to a distant world. The Corinthian menagerie, the lions, sphinxes, griffins, and so on, and their perfumes, wines, possibly clothes, and certainly helmets become part of the way in which the Etruscan elite differentiated themselves from the non-elite, and identified themselves with other elites, for this was increasingly an international aristocracy, mobile, intermarrying, and interdependent.

In order to house this activity, the Etruscans took up more space, lived more luxuriously, and represented themselves doing so, both in the large centres (where sadly the evidence is somewhat oblique) and in smaller settlements. Murlo is the best-known example, although exceptionally grand. Occupying a hill site (Poggio Civitate) near Siena, the site has a 7th and a 6th century phase, separated by a destruction level. To the earlier phase belonged an 8 × 35 m long building, with perhaps two storeys, and another at right angles to it, and these may have surrounded a courtyard. The roof was tiled and decorated with acroteria and antefixes, decorative features found on pediments and at the edges of tiled roofs—the earliest to have survived. Nearby was a tile workshop, which was destroyed in a fire—the footprints of people fleeing the conflagration across the drying tiles have been preserved. Terracottas include the ancient and eastern motif of the Mistress of the Animals (Potnia Theron), sphinxes, and horse and rider shapes. There was also metalwork—a cauldron seems to have had a fascinating group of two wrestlers and a referee.

In the 6th century the buildings were replaced with a complex of rooms around a courtyard some 60 × 62 m in size. A figure of a seated man with a beard and a tall hat, along with other human and fabulous animal statues, adorned the roof. Decorative friezes show banqueting with drinking and lyre-playing (and the first depiction of Etruscans reclining to dine in the Greek fashion, rather than sitting), seated figures, and chariot processions.

What was Murlo? Murlo may have been the home of a powerful family; or it might have been a ritual space where people gathered for celebrations—either way, it was completely destroyed and rendered inaccessible in the third quarter of the 6th century, a remarkable act of determined dismantlement. It is hard to know what one may take from Murlo that is genuinely applicable elsewhere, but at least it gives a sense of the scale at which the Etruscans could operate.

The clue to life in the larger settlements, which are less known archaeologically, comes from the necropoleis. The grandeur of the tumuli and their imposing architecture from the 7th century on is often thought to mirror the settlements—the cities of the dead imitating the cities of the living. The 7th and 6th centuries see both huge tombs, and a degree of infill. The variation which comes in suggests a society which is moving from a simple divide of rich and poor into a more nuanced stratification. It is very important to note that aspects of the 'oriental lifestyle' are found throughout; the richest graves are phenomenal, but quite poor graves still have some Greek pottery. We are reminded again that we do not necessarily see all of a population in a necropolis, but to some degree wealth penetrates Etruscan society.

One consequence of the introduction of writing and the techniques of display in funerary contexts was the emergence of inscriptions recording the names of the deceased, and as we have seen, this is another interesting indicator of the development of Etruscan society. The two-name system reflected a more sophisticated regime of property ownership and inheritance, a world in which it had become more important to pass wealth to one's descendants.

The exploitation of resources

Underpinning all this is the capacity of the Etruscans to exploit their abundant resources, and we can divide this into mineral resources and agriculture. Ancient settlements, with their pottery kilns and smelting, could be surprisingly 'industrial'. Populonia is the key site for the exploitation of the iron rich hills, but several cities developed highly skilled techniques. Vulci is noted for bronze sculpture; and other cities also have characteristic technologies—Volterra for alabaster for instance. Ceramic production is also highly specific; even when imitating Greek pottery, as Etruscans do, one can distinguish centres; and the famous bucchero ware so characteristic of the Etruscans shows distinctive forms and shapes depending on the place of production.

Thus the hard work of extraction was coupled with the fire of creative imagination in all Etruscan centres—but hard work it must have been, and dependent on substantial, well-organized labour forces. The same must have been true of agriculture. The classic Mediterranean trinity of oil, wine, and grain was produced in quantity in Etruria in the relatively fertile plains. Whilst individual landholdings are likely to have been small in the 8th to 6th centuries, the consumption patterns indicated by references to feasting and banqueting indicate production beyond subsistence levels. If the consequence of the Villanovan revolution had been to bring people from the countryside to the central settlements, the orientalizing period saw the infilling of the landscape once more, with evidence from small settlements to scattered graves. The landscape around Chiusi for instance is full of substantial and important tombs, which presumably indicate owners buried on their land. From the 8th to the 6th century we find developments up river valleys and across plains in a steadily rising trajectory. Again, labour must have been organized and controlled.

The mechanisms for such control are reflected in and were reinforced by the patterns of consumption and display discussed in this chapter. The most plausible model to explain the orientalizing period is that a culture already displaying a degree of social stratification and preparedness to exploit natural resource met, in the 8th century, a new and exciting set of opportunities to trade and to exchange, and to make a profit. Although there is no form of coinage, there are indications of various types of pre-monetary uses of metal. All this led to accelerated production of resource. The wealth flowing into settlements sustained increased competition and conspicuous consumption, which bolstered the position of the elite. New forms of dependency, new mechanisms of generosity, and new arenas of controlled conflict all drove forward the urban settlements, and the broader territory. The complexes at Piazza d'Armi at Veii and Vigna Parocchiale at Cerveteri for instance, constructed in the later 7th century preceding the temples of the following generations, were partly about religion but they may also have been steps in the construction of political control within communities; and territoriality must have become an issue as the boundaries of individual settlements were tested and established. The end result was expansion—the development of an Etruscan empire.

Chapter 6
Etruscan tomb painting and Etruscan art

Etruscan tomb painting looms large in any casual acquaintance with the Etruscans and their art, but was there a distinctive Etruscan artistic style, or should we think of more local phenomena? Can we say anything at all about the production of Etruscan art? What role did it have; was it merely decorative, or should we imbue the production and appreciation of Etruscan art with a greater sense of instrumental function?

To speak of Etruscan tomb painting (as indeed of Etruscan art) implies a relatively evenly spread occurrence (Figure 9). The phenomenon is actually very concentrated. About 180 paintings are known and of those some 140 are from Tarquinia; perhaps another 100 tombs simply have some traces of colour. Very few are found in northern Etruria. The earliest are in the furthest south—Veii and Cerveteri—but do not continue much past the 7th century. In Tarquinia, tomb painting starts in the 6th century and continues into the Hellenistic period (4th to 2nd centuries BC). At Chiusi, they are found during a brief period in the 5th century, elsewhere they are dated to the Hellenistic period, such as the 4th century tombs at Orvieto. Most Etruscan tomb painting is purely architectural.

The earliest tomb painting shares much with orientalizing art. A recently discovered example is the Tomb of the Roaring Lions at

9. A large single chambered tomb; three sarcophagi to left and right and a main sarcophagus in the centre, several decorated with painted processions. Dated to the late 4th and early 3rd centuries BC, the paintings are reminiscent of southern Italian tomb paintings. The family, the *Pinie*, are also attested at Vulci. The shield emblems are similar to emblems found on coinage of the time

Veii, currently the earliest tomb painting we know, dating to the later eighth or early seventh century BC. The lions come straight off the crude depictions on pottery and elsewhere; schematized, and slightly absurd, they are cauldrons with teeth, and one would not be remotely surprised if the artist had never seen a lion. This is in other words a clear transference from one art form to another.

Most early tomb painting shares these features; prowling, often fantastic animals, vegetation, and only occasionally human figures appear. If one places the iconography alongside occasional features like the seated statue figures at the Tomba delle Statue at Cerveteri, combining exotic sphinxes, lions, and the lavish architecture, it appears plain that we are here in a specific world of international aristocratic display, with a substantial interplay between elements, many of which were imported from other parts of the ancient world, including Greece and Phoenicia. This then is art as a marker of status. This was a language of power and to some degree of mysterious majesty, and those who projected the motifs of pottery and metalwork onto the walls of tombs were both imitators and innovators. The phenomenon may have been short-lived because it depended on a close relationship to specific orientalizing motifs which were outdated both artistically and socially by the 6th century.

The subsequent development of art within funerary contexts in Tarquinia is striking because it is so independent of other artistic forms. Although it recognizably reflects aspects of imported Greek pottery, it does so in a highly distinctive and free manner. This is art which is suited to its context and to the messages which it wishes to convey. Stylistic features also reflected Ionian art; the banquet, komos or revel, and grove are all features of the world of Dionysus. Satyrs and wineskins, sport and music all emphasize the world of play and contest which is also reflected—in Greece— in theatre and ritual. It has been suggested that this is the direct result of Ionian artists in Etruria, a phenomenon also seen in pottery production and in paintings on terracotta plaques in Cerveteri. Some of these show the judgement of Paris; his choice of Aphrodite over Hera and Athena would lead to his love for Helen and all the desperate events of the Trojan War that followed. The way that Aphrodite, unlike the others, has removed her long Etruscan dress to reveal her prominent breasts and shapely legs, may give a hint as to Paris's choice and his motivation. Greek influence is also alleged for terracotta decoration more generally. The story of Demaratus and his followers Eucheir (skilled hand), Diopos (keen eye), and Eugrammos (good designer) arriving from Corinth is part at least of a discourse of movement and mobility of artisans across the Mediterranean. However, recent work suggests that Italian developments are at least as early as anything we see in Greece, if not earlier.

Even if there are images which draw from Greek mythology, as we can see also on Etruscan mirrors, they seem highly independent of it. The Tomb of the Bulls at Tarquinia depicts Achilles waiting to ambush Troilos, whilst elsewhere a bull seems about to charge two men who are intimately engaged, and a cow looks out at us whilst a man and woman have sex behind her. Etruscan art tends to be less explicit than Greek art, so these are all the more striking. One sexual scene is on a terracotta jug from Cerveteri from around 600 BC, the Tragliatella oinochoe or wine jug, but it is part of a complex array of images. We also see a phalanx of soldiers, an exchange of gifts between a man and a woman, and two armed men on horseback (one with a monkey behind him) who might be interpreted as exiting a labyrinth, called Truia or Troy. Other images include a ship, a dog chasing a hare, and a woman pointing to two empty thrones. This is one of the most extreme indications of the independence of Etruscan art; the combination of motifs and ideas is original.

One way of distinguishing between Etruscan and Greek art is to explore the different ways in which reality and the imaginary world are depicted. In Etruscan art some of the boundaries seem to be deliberately blurred. It is often not clear in Tarquinian painting whether one is looking at a depiction of a real banquet or one in the afterlife or one in which humans and gods are both present, and the same has been suggested for some terracotta reliefs.

The Sarcophago degli Sposi from Cerveteri might be taken to represent some of these complexities. A major achievement in terracotta sculpture, and perhaps one of the most recognizable Etruscan images (there is another, perhaps by the same artist, in the Louvre), it was made in two halves because of its size. The sarcophagus represents a couple who recline together, each holding various objects now lost. The details of their braided hair, her hat and slippers, his beard, the pillow moulded into his resting arm are all justifiably praised—but who were they? They have the eyes and smiles of a Greek statue, but a totally different pose. He could be a bearded version of the Apollo from the temple roof of Veii—same braided hair and eyes. This is idealizing—perhaps it even hinted at the heroic nature of this now deceased couple?

From the 5th and 4th centuries, the imaginary is more highlighted in paintings, and the divide between worlds more clearly expressed. The imagery of Charun and the demons is distinctive and can be terrifying, whilst the deceased, where represented, is more realistically depicted. Sarcophagi place the mythology clearly on the base, and keep the humans very human. The taste for realism is clearly in place, with fat Etruscans, wrinkled Etruscans, old Etruscans, even old Etruscan couples, lying above depictions of highly theatrical scenes, such as the Seven against Thebes (Figures 14, 16). The influence of Greek art may be even greater. The sarcophagus of the Amazons, painted in tempera on limestone, is one of the most impressive examples of the application of Hellenistic realism in Etruria. The Amazons are fully clothed in long dresses in the Etruscan style, but a warrior who is about to die has the same level of realistic emotion as we see in the Alexander mosaic or other Greek pieces.

We have touched on the local differences in Etruscan art, and this can be brought into closer focus when one looks at other media. One of the most distinctive Etruscan productions is bucchero ware (Figure 10). The technique involved reducing the supply of oxygen in the kiln so that red ferric oxide in the clay becomes black ferric oxide (it is therefore dark grey throughout, not red with a black glaze as we see later). The clay was thoroughly levigated (its impurities removed) leaving a very fine fabric, which was burnished after firing. The vessels are often thought to imitate tarnished silver—they certainly share various shapes. This was a distinctive pottery form and was found throughout Etruria (somewhat heavier forms are more typical in the north) and exported widely.

10. Distinctive bucchero vessels with their elegant shapes, and fine
incised line or point decoration, were not only one of the most
common features of Etruscan burials, but were also a key export item

Terracotta production was also widespread and highly developed. Although marble existed in Etruria, and the marble from Luni (subsequently Carrara) was exploited by the Etruscans and especially by the Romans, limestone and terracotta are more typical as building materials. The so-called Tuscan order of column was typically very straightforward. With these materials, and the application of paint, Etruscan architecture must have been a riot of colour. Only occasionally—and often on the repetitive gorgons' heads or purely geometric decoration—do we see this colour surviving, but it was also applied to highly ornate pediments, with increasingly animated scenes. Lighter and capable of being produced in moulds, terracotta sculpture produced an art of emphatic repetition and of decorative luxury.

It may be that the success of working with moulds assisted the development of the remarkable Etruscan tradition of bronze sculpture, using the lost wax method. Whereas terracotta and ceramic is not reusable and so tends to survive in bulk, iron and bronze can be melted down and reused, and so rarely survives. Even so, there are some stunning pieces as early as the 8th century BC, when the Bisenzio trolley (in the Villa Giulia) was created, with a host of figures in different poses attached to a wheeled tripod. Much was purely utilitarian of course—and iron was substantially used for weaponry, whilst bronze was a common material for votive statuettes, ubiquitous in sanctuaries, and potentially having a quasi-monetary function before currency was introduced.

The larger pieces are characterized by extraordinary detail. The Arezzo Minerva, the so-called Orator, a fine over-life-size statue of a woman spinning from Vulci (based on a Greek original), and the ever-popular Chimera (also from Vulci) are the much reduced remains of a much larger production; in 1546, 6,000 pounds of ancient bronzes from Tarquinia were melted down to cover the columns in San Giovanni in Laterano (compare the 2,000 statues which the Romans are said to have taken from Volsinii in 265 BC). At Chianciano delle Terme, the museum preserves the meagre remains of what would have been a major bronze sculpture of figures in a horse-drawn chariot.

The major problem with this production however remains one of chronology. The recent discovery that the Capitoline Wolf, once thought to be an example of 5th century BC workmanship from Vulci, is in fact of medieval date (though some would now claim it is a medieval copy of an ancient original) shows how difficult this subject is. Nor can we really be sure how or where these monumental bronzes were displayed, but the later ones perhaps hint at the monumental decoration of public *fora*.

Bronze was also used for mirrors, their tang often inserted into decorated bone or ivory. Over 2,000 have survived, and their relief or incised decoration is a valuable source of information for mythology (Figure 11). They brought a world of imagery and storytelling into an intimate setting, and were clearly valuable—over time, they developed covers which protected the reflective part, and some are found in burials with that surface deliberately and poignantly destroyed.

Finally, one should mention the traditions of Etruscan jewellery. As befitted a world of luxury and display, the Etruscans imported and then constructed jewellery of striking beauty. One classic form is the fibula, or brooch; in essence a beautified safety pin. They could be in many materials—some combined metal with bone, amber, or another metal. Ingenious designs were created, but the most splendid were in gold.

The Etruscans developed many ways of using gold. We see gold leaf, with patterns pressed in from behind; solid or hollow gold tubes, sometimes decorated with gold wire (filigree) or granulation. The latter technique has fascinated scholars—it appears that the Etruscans used copper salt with an animal or

11. Mirrors were often incised with Greek myths; this one from the 5th century BC shows Aphrodite visiting Helen, and perhaps persuading her to follow Paris to Troy. Other myths appear to be more local, either indigenous stories, or local versions of Greek myths

mineral resin to produce a firm adhesive at a relatively low temperature. These decorations can be purely geometric, or representational, often of animals, and in the finest examples the decoration is incredibly dense and rich. Gold could be applied to a variety of other materials, including silver, to produce even more valuable objects; some of these were used to decorate furniture. Bracelets and earrings are common, as are necklaces, often with a series of different pendants. Many Etruscans of both sexes wore rings, and many rings had a gem with an incised device, which was sometimes used as a seal. The richness of imagination and skill in producing gems in various semi-precious stones is a subject all to its own. The most breathtaking are the diadems with leaves rendered in gold in great detail. This jewellery often borrowed from Greek models, but the Etruscans had great skill in this area, and continued working in gold into the 3rd century, when we begin to see a reduction in evidence for luxury in tombs.

The central fascination of Etruscan art remains that it is clearly immensely indebted to Greek originals, but it is also capable of great independence. This has sometimes been held against it; one interpretation would make of Etruscan art a sort of second rate barbaric failure to reach the same heights as the Greeks. That interpretation depends on the assumption that either in their artistic taste or their functional approach to the messages of Greek art, the Etruscans were seeking the same effects and the same style. The evidence suggests that in fact the Etruscans were using the artistic ideas they received to do different things, and that the messages may have been different.

We are disadvantaged by the loss of any substantial evidence from areas other than tombs or temples, but ideas of luxury, display, symbols of status, and a joy in decoration seem to be undeniable. Moreover, the orientalizing period encouraged a trend of representing key ideas in artistic form. Narrative is an important part of sarcophagi, temple decoration, and tomb painting, and although over time the narratives become more stereotypical and less imaginative or unexpected, in the 6th to 4th centuries BC, the Etruscans have a highly developed repertoire of imagery and ornamentation to draw upon.

How far this art actually determined the thought patterns of those who were wearing these stories, or finding them on the backs of their mirrors, or glimpsing them in tombs, and knowing that one day they too would come to share this image world, is not recoverable directly. The variation between different centres of production hints at a sensibility towards the relationship between material and message. Partly by reason of archaeological recovery but substantially because of the sheer quantity, Etruscan artistic production really does stand out in Italy. The amount of bucchero, iron, bronze, gold, and silver which was clearly produced and in circulation is a critical part of the distinctiveness of Etruria in its heyday. For the Etruscans, the production of art was both an economically successful strategy, and also a culturally important marker. By consuming and producing work of high quality and prestige at such a level, the Etruscans were making claims about their position in a world which they shared with Greeks and Phoenicians, and to whom they seem reluctant to have ceded any sense of superiority.

Chapter 7
Empire, crisis, and response, 600–300 BC

The orientalizing period was one of immense innovation and success. By 600 BC, the Etruscans were the most prosperous and successful of the Italic peoples, and in the period covered by this chapter, Etruscan art achieved some of its most iconic and well-known moments, in tomb painting and sculpture. Yet this was also a period of tension and unrest, which would end in political decline. One of the fascinations of Etruscan society is how to understand its art and culture within the context of its political evolution, a historicized reading rather than a parade of stunning images. For although the loss of any relevant literary evidence from the Etruscans themselves leaves us in difficulties when it comes to understanding their civil society, the archaeology hints at a complex and intriguing set of approaches to their political life. One of the reasons why the Etruscans are historically significant is because they give hints and indications of the alternative paths taken by city-states and cultures in antiquity. As we proceed, Rome will enter definitively into this history, with its radically different—and astonishingly successful—ideologies.

The city-states of southern Etruria, Veii, Cerveteri, Tarquinia, Vulci, Orvieto, are the most advanced. Fortification walls, monumental tombs, substantial housing, and the first stone built temples characterize the architecture, whilst control of territory is signalled by substantial occupation of the territory coupled with satellite settlements such as Pyrgi and Gravisca. This advanced organization of territory was accompanied by shifts in the nature of political control.

Orientalizing culture was fundamentally aristocratic, but it may also have been somewhat like the closed aristocracies of Greek city-states such as Corinth; intermarrying but without a single specific leader. By the 6th century there are indications of what scholars sometimes call kings, representing a very clear shift in political control towards sole power and monarchy.

However this may not be a sign of stability. Although there are some highly successful families—the Tolumnii at Veii for instance—it is not clear that all kingships were hereditary. Nor should we make too many inferences from the modern word 'king'. The chief magistrate of an Etruscan city seems to have been the *lucumo*, but the functions of that individual may have been highly ritualized and sacerdotal; in particular the office is associated with the meeting of the cities' representatives to the Etruscan League which took place at Fanum Voltumnae near Orvieto. However, other individuals and other magistracies may have had more power too. In Rome, and in parts of the Greek world, the retention of a highly traditional magistracy for purely ritual purposes is attested, whilst more politicized offices took over some of their functions.

Issues of control and authority must have been a matter of concern because Etruria was also becoming more militarily sophisticated. The Etruscans were developing a form of warfare which was similar to Greek warfare. Each individual was more heavily armoured than before, with a shield, sword, and lance, and the numbers involved may have been on the increase. This form of warfare (sometimes called 'hoplite' from the Greek, *hoplon* being the typical round shield) was still associated with strongly hierarchical social forms; indeed the Etruscans were perhaps deploying the very limited form of hoplite warfare depicted on vases such as the Chigi or Aristonothos vases, not the mass participation which became the norm in the 5th century in Athens and Sparta. The elite may have retained their chariots (just as the cavalry remained significant even in Greece, where arguments have often been made about the apparently equalizing and democratic consequences of hoplite warfare). Yet larger armies required both stronger forms of civic ideology and the mechanisms for control.

The architecture which was the backdrop to these social developments was also changing. Houses developed in size and sophistication; often around a courtyard and incorporating columns, tiled roofs, and terracotta decorations. An element of orthogonal or rectilinear street-planning in towns may be reflected in the more regular tombs at Cerveteri and Orvieto, which are squared and in rows. The northern Etruscan settlement of Marzabotto adopted a rigidly orthogonal town grid in the late 6th or early 5th century.

Some of the very richest burials in Etruria and central Italy generally belong to the period around 625 BC. Extraordinary levels of gold, silver, and luxury objects from far afield accompanied some burials; Vulci had a particularly strong centre of production of high quality metalwork too. This level of deposition begins to tail off in the 6th century, although not completely and it should also be noted that tombs become more elaborately painted and decorated in the 6th century. One cannot straightforwardly conclude that Etruscan society was becoming poorer, but it does appear that it was changing, that extreme acts of aristocratic display in the funerary context were diminishing, and that more people may have been involved in successful commerce.

Self-regulation of elite behaviour is also found in other parts of central Italy and in parts of Greece. For whilst display is one very important aspect of the ways in which individuals could dominate, it was also a mechanism for inciting envy and it was ultimately self-directed, and a funeral lasted for a short while. If we are right to suggest that the Etruscans were pressing towards more communal activity, investment in representations of long-lasting civic value may have had more impact. It is from this period that the number of magistracies appears to increase, suggesting a more complex political life; and it is in the 6th century that we see the development of monumental stone built temples, and the practices of repetitive deposition within them, which offer new and different ways of demonstrating status and authority.

The port sites of Pyrgi and Gravisca give a clue into the processes at work. They may have been unusual settlements in a way, because their function was to be a place of interaction between peoples, including non-Etruscans; and trading centres were set up around the Mediterranean to permit a degree of intermixing which may have been less welcome inland—Al Mina in Phoenicia and Naukratis in Egypt spring to mind. It has been suggested that Etruscan settlements were more open to non-Italians in the 7th than in the 6th centuries, so that these settlements were a way of maintaining exchange but isolating it from the main city. However, we should not underestimate how much mobility there was by Etruscans between Etruscan settlements, or from Etruria to Campania (as attested at Pontecagnano and Capua), or across central Italy. At Volsinii (Orvieto) in the 7th and 6th centuries BC we find burials of Achilena and Perecele (probably the Greek names Achilles and Pericles); at Cerveteri we find a Roman Fabius, and a Titus Latinus at Veii; at Tarquinia we find Rutilus Hippokrates (a Latin first name and a Greek second name); and the Katacinus at Volsinii might have been a Celt. Nearly 100 Attic vases from the later 6th century bear the mark of the trader Sostratos from Aegina who is mentioned by the Greek historian Herodotus as having made a fortune, and it may even be his on a stone anchor from Gravisca, whilst we now have an inscription on a bucchero amphora of an Etruscan dedicating in the sanctuary of Aphaia at Aegina, which shows movement in both directions.

A characteristic function and need of these centres was to create a climate of confidence. Since trade was being actively sought and was absolutely essential to the lubrication of the social and economic life of the larger and more populous cities, it was necessary to demonstrate fairness, and security. It is unsurprising therefore to see a strong religious element in both Pyrgi and Gravisca, with the introduction of deities especially from the Greek world and objects which related to measurement. These sites were developing as sophisticated trading posts and were highly connected; the same names occur on objects in Gravisca and in Naukratis, objects made in Naukratis are deposited in Gravisca, and the flow of Egyptianizing or Egyptian objects into Etruria was now significant, though the carriers may have been largely Greek. Indeed Pyrgi was a sanctuary of international status.

These and other centres, such as the Forum Boarium at Rome, were transformative. The ideas which they brought from the Greek world (itself undergoing major political and social change) may have intensified the political development of the cities. The replacement in the 6th century of Corinthian pottery with its relatively generic depictions by Attic pottery with its highly specific references to Greek myth and epic may have accelerated the syncretism of Etruscan religious belief with Greek models. It is from the 6th century that one can see the Etruscans representing their deities in Greek ways, although interestingly the Etruscans became experts in the use of terracotta and their exploitation of marble was limited. One intriguing exception is the statuette of a nude goddess from a sanctuary within the Cannicella necropolis at Orvieto. It is an imported Greek sculpture, 73 cm in height. It is—most unusually for Etruria—nude, and it is a puzzling piece which was recarved locally to take a gold diadem.

Contemporaneously we see substantial Etruscan expansion both southwards and northwards. Is it possible that direct contact with the Greeks encouraged a more aggressive territorial approach?

Or was it simply the necessity of increasing commerce to satisfy growing demand which drove the Etruscans into a period of imperialism?

The two experiences turned out very differently. The southern adventure was a disaster; the northern expansion far more successful, perhaps fuelled by the loss of the southern markets. Etruscans moved strongly and successfully into the north, areas which were perhaps relatively underpopulated. Orvieto and Chiusi were probably the prime movers; Volterra, Fiesole, and Perugia were also involved. We have already mentioned the highly regular city of Marzabotto, which interestingly seems to have taken its measurements from the Greek standard. It was built for convenience, with wells, stepping stones in the streets, well-equipped houses, and its main temple was neatly fitted into the town plan. Largely a productive centre, it also gives us a warning about the dangers of reading directly from necropoleis to urban centres, since—in contrast to the neat regularity of the city—the necropoleis of Marzabotto are somewhat irregular in plan.

Spina on the Adriatic harbour was a port site, founded around 500 BC at the same time as Marzabotto. It was a desperately problematic site—frequently flooded, the houses were built on piles and, like an ancient Venice, the inhabitants may have used waterways instead of streets. The necropoleis show a wealthy population with a lot of bronze vessels, gaming pieces, and dice. Men and women have similar levels of wealth; and Attic pottery is found in very substantial quantities, and appears to have been brought by Athenians, who are attested by inscriptions alongside a diverse group of Etruscans from Perugia, Chiusi, and Bologna. Spina's wealth and internationalism was so great that, like Cerveteri and unlike any other Etruscan city, it had a treasury in the sanctuary of Apollo at Delphi.

Another new settlement was Pisa. Pisa's position on the Arno was vital for its commercial success; it was another port site of course.

It has a longer history than some of the others mentioned here; it probably started in the middle 7th century, and rapidly developed sanctuaries and necropoleis with a startling array of material; equally impressive is the export of Pisan material, bucchero, impasto, and marble. The expansion up the western coast of Italy led to southern France. Pisan material is dominant at Genoa for instance, and further north, as we can see at the settlement of Lattes near Montpellier in the Languedoc. This site is an indication of how important Etruscan and Pisan influence was in an area where the main settlement was the Greek colony of Massilia (Marseille). Indications of the extraordinary vitality of this trade in the 6th century include sites like Saint-Blaise or Lattes, where Etruscan amphorae competed with Massilian products. The hundreds of sherds demonstrate a deep connection, and one which perhaps rested on longer-term trading for metals, salt, and slaves. It was an organized trade, and it was international, as is shown by a 5th century inscription on lead from the site of Pech-Maho, a site with a strong Iberian influence. There was an Etruscan inscription, which may refer to a Massilian, but the lead has been reused for a Greek inscription about a complex commercial transaction involving securities.

This therefore is a trading empire of some complexity, in which individual cities have strong parts to play. Yet a debate has recently begun about whether one can or should speak of colonization in the Etruscan context (more or less at the same time as Greek historians worry about whether it is appropriate in the Greek context), and outside Italy, it is difficult to see any exclusively Etruscan settlements. It might be safer to say that the Etruscans display both mobility and a developed concept of territorial control, including controlling the sea, through what has been called a 'non-colonial thalassocracy'. Whilst none of these ventures may have been exclusively the action of one city, they are also not, as far as we can tell, communal 'Etruscan' initiatives. The northern expansion may have been in response to the failure of the southern cities; it did not look to involve them.

The relationship between Etruria and Campania is much harder to understand in some ways. There were close cultural relationships between the two regions, and sites like Pontecagnano had a strong cultural assemblage which looked very much like the Villanovan of Etruria. The relationship between Etruria and Pontecagnano and Capua was long-standing and deep (although the material record is different in the two Campanian towns, so they may have been connected with different parts of Etruria). Interaction can be traced back to the 9th century, and seems continuous, although both sites, now increasingly well known from their thousands of burials, also developed their own distinctive artistic forms. However there was a further upsurge of activity in the 7th and 6th centuries, and it is the nature of this second wave that concerns us now.

Inscriptions show the presence of Etruscans, and there is strikingly fine bronzework, bucchero, and pottery painted in an Etruscan style (predominantly animals, banquets, and games). This successful interpenetration of culture needs to be understood with care. Are these wholly Etruscan settlements? Probably not. The sources hint that the Etruscans formed an elite within Capua at least. So we may need a different model for how the Etruscans operated in these settlements.

The sources for the Etruscan presence in Campania are poor, so we need to look elsewhere for models, and one place to look is the relationship between Etruria and Rome. We have a lot of information about early Rome in our sources, but it is not entirely reliable, and it was all written much later than the events. The first Roman to have written a history was Fabius Pictor in around 200 BC (little of it survived). So how good was their information? At least some seems to have come down as stories, possibly in dramatic form, but the apparently stable and secure account which the Roman historian Livy gives us for the period of the kings at Rome (753 to 509 BC) is the product of much complicated writing and rewriting, and not nearly as certain as it might appear. Even the Romans worried about their early history, with Livy pointing out that many of the relevant documents must have been destroyed in the sack of Rome by the Gauls in 390 BC.

The story of Aeneas coming from the east to land in Italy is related to the Trojan War epic and was not a story that belonged solely to Rome, and it is independent of the story of Romulus and Remus founding the city. That story is found in many different versions, not all of them with the twins. Moreover, the account of two babies set off in a tiny boat to float down the Tiber to land at Rome, where they would be suckled by a wolf, is tremendously exciting, but not historical.

Modern historians of early Rome have substantial difficulties therefore, but some have thought that these reduce when one arrives at the last three kings of Rome, the first of whom is an Etruscan: Tarquinius Priscus. Tarquinius was said to be the son or grandson of a Corinthian named Demaratus. He was an exile from the overthrow of the Bacchiad aristocracy in the mid-7th century, and was said to have brought his craftsmen with him, who introduced Corinthian pottery techniques to the Etruscans. His son was called Lucumo, which simply means king, and he changed his name to Lucius when he moved from Tarquinia to Rome. Lucius Tarquinius then had followed many other aristocrats (including his father) in moving from one city to another to find favour. Assiduous in self-promotion and supported by an ambitious wife, Tanaquil, Tarquinius persuaded the Romans to make him king after Ancus Marcius.

It is worth very briefly outlining the next stages in the history for context. According to the sources, Tarquinius reigned for 38 years, and was successful in expanding Roman territory. He was succeeded by Servius Tullius, who was variously thought to be the child of a slave woman who miraculously conceived after seeing a phallus in a hearth, or the son of one of the leaders of a city which Tarquinius had conquered, or an Etruscan. Servius Tullius brought in a number of popular reforms, and transformed the Roman constitution, but Tarquinius' son or grandson, with the same name, schemed with Servius' own daughter to bring a brutal end to the reign (Tullia is said to have driven over her father's body in her chariot, a grisly detail which fits with the evidence for women being buried with chariots). The younger Tarquinius was more unpleasant than his predecessor, and gained the nickname the Proud (Superbus). He was successful in war, but contemptuous of the proper limits of power and his son raped the virtuous Lucretia, kinswoman of one Junius Brutus. Lucretia committed suicide; Brutus swore vengeance; and Tarquinius and his family were expelled from Rome in 509 BC, and the Republic established. (Some 450 years later, Brutus' relative Marcus Brutus was reminded of his ancestor's bravery and determination, and found the courage to lead the plot against the quasi-king Julius Caesar.)

In comparison with the previous period, the reigns of the last three kings seem quite sharply focused, with lots of details and plenty of family intrigue. Yet it is precisely the soap-opera-like nature of the literary account which renders it troubling. What can Rome's story really tell us about the Etruscans?

The amount of archaeological material inspired by the Etruscans but found in Roman contexts is substantial; bucchero and Etrusco-Corinthian pottery, metalwork, inscriptions, including dedications in sanctuaries. There was even a Tuscan quarter in the city (the vicus Tuscus, leading from the Forum to the Circus Maximus). In 1936, Giorgio Pasquale coined the phrase La Grande Roma dei Tarquini, and the assumption grew that upstart Rome was heavily influenced by the more sophisticated Etruscans. Much Roman religion was derived from the Etruscans, but it was thought that the Romans also learnt the concept of the triumph, gladiatorial games, even many of their crafts. That of course could not be the work of one man. So Tarquinius came to be seen as a literary reflection of a much larger takeover of Rome. The sources in other words had systematically downplayed the extent of Etruscan domination by focusing on just the king.

So the combination of the apparent downplaying of Etruscan influence, the archaeological material, and a belief that somehow the Romans needed others to kickstart their development led to the theory that the Etruscans dominated Rome during the period of the last three kings, and must therefore have been present in much greater numbers. If this were so, it would give us a particular model of the way the Etruscans took over cities, and one might imagine something similar in Campania.

However, Rome and Campania were different. The vast majority of inscriptions in the Campanian cities of Capua, Nola, Suessula, Pompeii, and Pontecagnano are in Etruscan, but only a fraction of Roman inscriptions for the same time. There is no reason to doubt that the Romans did indeed borrow substantially from the Etruscans, but no reason to overstate that either. There is also an issue of scale; on most interpretations, Rome was larger than most of the Campanian cities. The relationship between Etruria and Rome was one of interaction, and some population movement at an elite end. The relationship between Etruria and Campania looks different, maybe because the Etruscans were for a certain period of time much the largest of the non-Campanian groups in the cities.

Finally, we should acknowledge that the interactions between all these cultures were more complex than we might care to admit. One of the most remarkable correspondences between literary evidence and archaeological evidence comes in the comparison between a 4th century BC painting in Vulci, from the so-called François tomb, and a speech made by emperor Claudius in AD 48 and recorded on a bronze tablet in Lyon. From this speech we learn that Etruscan sources claimed that Servius Tullius was not the son of a prisoner of war, but a companion of Caeles Vibenna (whom Claudius Latinizes as Caelius Vivenna). His Etruscan name was

Mastarna. At some stage he left Etruria with Caelius' army and occupied the Caelian hill at Rome, changed his name to Servius, and became king.

In the François tomb we find two painted scenes, in one of which Trojan prisoners are about to be sacrificed by Greeks at the funeral of Achilles' friend Patroclus (a scene which is described in the *Iliad*); in the other, armed men, several naked, slaughter unarmed opponents, some clothed. The individuals are named. The victorious side include Avle and Caile Vipinas and Macstrna; the defeated include Cneve Tarchunies Rumach (Gnaeus Tarquinius from Rome); Laris Papathnas Velznach (perhaps from Volsinii); and Pesna Arcmsnas Sveamach (possibly from Sovana). One interpretation which has found favour has the Vibennas and Macstrna as captives, who are released by one of their own side, Larth Ulthes; one by one they release each other and kill their captors who appear to have fallen asleep.

That the Vibenna brothers existed and were well-known adventurers appears secure; in the first half of the 6th century, Avile Vipiiennas dedicates a bucchero vase at Veii. The scene may have reflected some raid or adventure—we cannot locate it to any particular place. The unfortunate band are being slaughtered as inevitably as the Trojans—it is interesting that this leaves the Vulcentines taking the role of the Greeks. Is Gnaeus Tarquinius of Rome Tarquinius Priscus? It is not clear—the usual praenomen was Lucius, and no other source has him killed by Servius. As for Macstrna, the unusual use of a single name instead of the usual two names hints at a nickname or a title—is it a version of *magister*, of which at Rome there was both a *magister populi* and a *magister equitum*? Then Servius Tullius would be the given name of someone who held an office, just as Lucius Tarquinius was the name of a man who held the office of Lucumo.

Claudius' version of events, which he ascribed to Etruscan sources, is incompatible with the Latin account. It also introduces the clear expectation that movement of individuals was accompanied by their supporters, a phenomenon we also see described when Claudius' ancestor, Attus Clausus, early in the 5th century BC was said to have left the Sabina with all his family and supporters and moved to Rome. This mobility, coupled with the determined pursuit of power and display of military prowess, gives a rather more jagged and violent image of the interplay between cities and their elites. Yet any group who came to Rome had to work within the large population there. We may see traces of the succession of such leaders; in Campania, for a period of time, the Etruscans may have simply been more dominant. That dominance however would not last.

The ultimate reason perhaps was the competition within the Mediterranean, itself once more sparked off by problems further east. When the Phocaean Greeks were attacked by the Persians, it was obvious that they would turn to the sea. They had already founded a colony at Marseille, and were operating as far afield as the Guadalquivir valley in Spain. They endeavoured to find a new home and their objective was Corsica, but the idea of a new band of marauders settled on a strategically important island, and one which had had close links with Etruria, was unpalatable not only to Etruria but also to the Carthaginians. They too would feel the cold wind from the east; Cyrus conquered Phoenicia and many emigrated to Carthage. Perhaps the Carthaginians already recognized that an increased population would require a closer grip of the western Mediterranean. It is noteworthy that Carthaginians and Etruscans were working out a modus vivendi; Polybius, the Greek historian who recounts the conflicts between Rome and Carthage in the 3rd and 2nd centuries BC, gives us vital information about a sequence of treaties between the two parties, and a bilingual inscription in Punic and Etruscan in Pyrgi from around 500 BC attests the same formal relations.

It was around 540 BC that the Carthaginians and the Etruscans combined to defeat the Phocaeans and expelled them from the area around Corsica; they made their way south to Rhegium in Calabria. It was a vital but costly victory. The captured Phocaeans were divided between the Carthaginians and the people of Cerveteri (Agylla in Greek); the Etruscans stoned their prisoners to death. This act was followed by a period of disease and famine, and the city applied to Delphi for advice—exactly as a Greek city would—and obeyed the commands. Clearly by the middle of the 6th century, Cerveteri knew exactly how to behave from one point of view, and yet that capacity to work within the contexts of Greek religious behaviour did not prevent the Etruscans from also pursuing an aggressive policy, securing parts of Corsica, Sardinia, and the Lipari islands.

This carving out of different areas of influence turned into a direct attack on a Greek city in Campania, Cumae. The reasons are obscure. The sources tell us that in 524 BC, the Etruscans led a vast army of Umbrians, Daunians, and many other allies, and attribute the reason to pressure on the Etruscans' northern possessions from the Gauls. The story is implausible at many levels—the Gauls made little impact. The huge forces deployed are surely exaggerated. Connections with Daunia to the south of Campania did exist; various sites show Etruscan metalwork and bucchero; Ruvo has a superb collection of luxury goods including ivory and gold; Ruvo, Arpi, Canosa, and Egnazia have tomb paintings with a strong Etruscan influence; and everywhere in the area closest to Campania we find Etruscan antefixes with nimbi, or haloed heads (as opposed to antefixes with Greek-style gorgons' heads) on the new stone-built temples. Yet there was little to motivate a vast army, nor indeed any hint of previous difficulty. This unsuccessful and ultimately self-defeating act has been written up by later, or local, sources.

There may have been an attempt like the sort of military adventure depicted in the François tomb. However, Cumae was well defended and in battle Aristodemus stood out; his prowess brought him popular favour. This undertow of popular versus aristocratic tension resurfaces time and again; when Lars Porsenna sent his son Aruns to Aricia to defeat the Latin city there, they appealed to Cumae. The government sent Aristodemus with such a poor force that they were clearly hoping for his defeat, but instead he won and returned to even greater fame, and to take sole rule. Intriguingly, he later became heir to the Tarquins, and whereas Cumae had supported Rome with supplies of grain when Rome was under pressure from Lars Porsenna, such help was refused in 492 (yet given by other Etruscans).

Allegedly Aristodemus introduced great luxury into the city, encouraging young men to wear their hair in ringlets and use hair nets and perfume and long robes. This was allegedly intended to sap their manly spirit, but probably means an influx of Etruscan habits and an upsurge in affluence dependent on strong agricultural production, which was said to have been achieved by forcing young nobles to till the fields. In the end, these young nobles and other Cumaeans in exile in Capua joined forces, broke into the city, tortured Aristodemus and his family cruelly to death, and restored aristocratic government. (In another version reported by Plutarch in his stories of female virtue, Aristodemus wears the Cumaeans out by forcing them to build a canal. As he passes by a woman veils her face, and when asked by her male friends why she did this only for him, she replies that it was because Aristodemus was the only man in Cumae. This shames the men and encourages Aristodemus' concubine Xenocrita to betray him.)

With these highly wrought and entertaining stories we have passed far from the sober world of archaeological inference. How does this help us understand the nature of Etruscan influence in Campania? It would not be surprising if there were a local tradition about such a larger than life figure, and Cumae, as a Greek colony, was accessible to Greek historians. Many of the stories follow standard patterns; the attempt to exhaust the Cumaeans by building works has an exact parallel with the

Tarquins at Rome. Little in the accounts justifies belief in blocks of consistently cooperating states however. In Cumae especially we see a deep division between a presumably Greek elite and the local population, and it is interesting that in opposition, it is Etruscan customs which are championed. If we think in terms of competing aristocracies and dashing adventurers, we may be closer to the mark, and the Etruscan dominance in Campania appears cultural. That would not diminish its effectiveness and significance. As allegiances shifted back and forth, it is interesting that Rome could be seen as both ally and villain. Cumae may not have wanted a strong Rome under an Etruscan king, but it does not seem to have wanted a strong Rome under a Republic either. An uneasy set of equilibria were being sustained, until the death of Aristodemus seems to have made Cumae once more a target.

In 474, again for reasons we cannot recover, the Etruscans attacked, with the Carthaginians. Cumae appealed to Hieron, tyrant of Syracuse, who lent his fleet. The victory was huge. Hieron dedicated helmets inscribed with his name at the temple of Zeus in Olympia. The Greek poet Pindar, in a hymn written in 470 in honour of Hieron after he had won a chariot race at the Pythian games in Delphi, fashioned this victory into an equal to the Athenian and Spartan victories over the Persians at Salamis and Plataea; may the war cry of the Phoenicians and the Etruscans be silent, the singer prays, now that they have seen at Cumae that their aggression destroyed their fleet, when the leader of the Syracusans hurled their youth from their swift ships into the sea and 'delivered Hellas from grievous slavery'.

This is overstated, and one might argue instead that Cumae had given the pretext for Syracuse to begin its campaign of hegemony. Under powerful leaders, with a massive fleet, and capable of withstanding Carthage and defeating the onslaught of Athens when the Peloponnesian War spilt over into Sicily, Syracuse was a formidable force. That however is a different story, and whilst the defeat of the Etruscans—probably again largely the southern coastal cities—may have been damaging to a degree, it is not clear that it was the critical factor in the decline of Etruscan influence in Campania.

For that, we must look to the new force in Italian politics, the tribes of Oscan speaking Samnites from the central Apennines. Capua was conquered in 423 BC and Cumae in 421, but these events are the outcome of long-drawn-out population movements and internal change which brought waves of settlers down into the coastal plains. The Latins had their own difficulties with the Volscians, Aequians, and Hernicans, groups obscure even by the 1st century BC, but a terrifying reality in the 5th century, as we can see from the complete change of burial practice at the Latin site of Satricum when it is taken over. Language shift is another sign of population movement; Oscan displaces Etruscan. At Pompeii, we see changes in settlement pattern, and language, and the titles of magistrates. The figure of the warrior becomes ubiquitous in art.

Thus Campania added yet another linguistic and cultural group to its history. With a strong Etruscan influence visible in its Villanovan culture, a fringe of Greek colonies, a second phase of Etruscan influence, and then an Oscan presence which was clearly highly forceful, this was an area in which multiple overlapping identities coexisted. It was interestingly factional, and native, Etruscan, and Greek identities can all be traced. With the arrival of the Oscans however, it is the Etruscan identity which disappears.

Defeated in the south, and effectively invisible in Campania from the later 5th century BC, the Etruscans were soon to experience yet another setback in their northern territories. The story told by the sources (which are inconsistent) and the reality are probably at odds. Livy illustrates the problem. The question that required to be answered was what brought the Gauls to sack Rome, around 390 BC. A popular answer blamed the whole thing on one Etruscan, Arruns of Clusium (Chiusi). Arruns looks after the son of a man called Lucumo; when the ungrateful boy grows up, he rapes Arruns's wife, and shames her publicly. Arruns heads north, meets the Gauls, shows them the wonderful produce of the plains of Etruria, and entices them south. Once they arrived they proved to be less manageable than foolish Arruns had expected. Livy himself points out that this story cannot have been right. The Gauls had already crossed the Alps. Maybe the people of Chiusi, or someone there, had been the cause of the southern movement, but the story goes back further. Livy blames the Massilians—it was they, in the time of Tarquinius Priscus, who lured the Gauls across the Alps, and for 200 years the Etruscans had been facing the northern challenge. The real likelihood is that they may have had an offer to fight as mercenaries in southern Italy.

The archaeological evidence supports Livy's second answer, but also suggests that the Etruscans had very satisfactorily managed the relationship. The Gauls had for some time before they crossed the Alps been using Etruscan goods; as we have seen there are good reasons for supposing close relations between Villanova and the Urnfeld culture. The importance of settlements such as Bologna, Spina, and Marzabotto either preceded or survived the first waves of Gallic incomers, and they may in fact have become even more assimilated to Etruscan culture. However, the 5th and 4th century pushes were more problematic, disrupting inland regions and the north-east (Raetia and the Veneto), transforming Bologna, and possibly affecting Pisa. Once the route across the Alps was open, there was always the possibility of new movements. It is interesting that Gallic culture tended to encourage dispersed settlement, as on the other side of the Alps, and ultimately this would make the area much weaker when the Romans came north themselves.

Taken as a whole we have seen a 6th century move into northern Italy, which remained largely successful until the later 4th century, when the Gallic pressure grew; and a long-term engagement with Campania, revived again in the 6th century, but challenged and in the 5th century overturned. We have also seen that this was in no discernible sense a concerted effort by all the Etruscans; it is a series of endeavours by individual city-states or groups, and in some cases it may reflect quite isolated acts of banditry.

It is therefore difficult to speak of an Etruscan empire, in the way that one can of the Roman empire. On the other hand, we should not underplay the success of the Etruscans across the majority of Italy. From southern France through Liguria, across to the Veneto in one direction and Corsica in the other, and down to Lucania, Etruscan goods and Etruscan influence was felt for two centuries, and offered standards of behaviour and luxury which had lasting impact. Dashing as the Etruscan nobility no doubt could be on the battlefield, and experienced as their fleet must have been at sea, the abiding image one has of the Etruscans is as traders and effective ambassadors for their own cultural package.

In the 7th and 6th centuries, Etruscan cities and Etruscan individuals were part of a connected trade network in which a multiplicity of objects could be exchanged. Notions of fairness and equity sat alongside ruthlessness and piracy. Steady agricultural exploitation supplied the wine and oil and other commodities that filled the amphorae or containers, and were consumed in mixing bowls or from plates and cups. In the 5th century, competition for markets was clearly intense, and the Etruscans lose ground—at the southern French sites like Saint Blaise, Etruscan material dwindles as a proportion of the discovered amphorae.

What impact did these vicissitudes have on Etruria itself? We have already seen that the major necropoleis seem to have included a broader range of individuals, and represented a more commercial class. In the 5th century though there is a real sense of a reduction in activity in the major old Etruscan centres, although as ever there are exceptions; Populonia seems to go from strength to strength, and is notable for its coinage. By the 5th and 4th centuries, many Etruscan cities were producing their own coinage.

The answer may have varied from city-state to city-state. Tarquinia and Volsinii have been thought to have maintained a sternly oligarchic approach; the tomb painting of Tarquinia becomes rather conservative, and the extraordinary regularity of tombs in the necropolis of Crocefisso del Tufo at Orvieto may suggest a very strong central authority. At Veii the rise and fall of the Tolumnii suggests a different pattern, as does the evidence from Pyrgi.

At Pyrgi, the gold tablets which refer to relations between Carthage and Cerveteri are found in the context of a sanctuary which has a highly international flavour (see Figure 4). The deity worshipped is perhaps most easily related to the Punic deity Astarte. Yet the extraordinary pedimental frieze on another temple showing the moment where Tydeus eats the brains of his defeated enemy Melanippus seems to have more than usual significance (Figure 12). The key figure in the Pyrgi texts is an individual called Thefarie Velianas, who holds the office of MLK in Punic, and *zilaθ* for the third time in Etruscan. This odd mix of a Phoenician kingship with an Etruscan annual magistracy, the reference to the favour of Uni/Astarte, the trappings of something extraordinary reflected in the tablets themselves, suggests rather the kind of individual charismatic power we see in a Tarquin, or in a Greek tyrant. It may be that at Cerveteri, the combination of changing social dynamics, the internal and external pressures of the late 6th century, and the allure of Carthaginian models, encouraged an attempt at extraordinary individual power. A generation later, the frieze on Temple A seems to have warned against hubris and the dangers of excess. Temple A can then be read as a commentary on Thefarie Velianas's rule, and part of the fluid and unsettled politics of the time.

The relative introspection of the Etruscans in the 5th and 4th centuries is unsurprising. Caught between the internal pressures of societies which had grown fast, and where power was limited to

12. This reconstruction shows a moment from the story of the Seven against Thebes, on which Tydeus is overcome with anger and eats the brains of his defeated enemy Melanippus. The gods look on in horror. From temple A, around 470/60 BC

a̱ few but was being demanded by more, and external challenges both to the north and the south, and in the Mediterranean sea, the Etruscans were bound to have felt some impact. For instance, the Pyrgi tablets also give weight to the possibility that Rome and Carthage had a treaty as early as 509 BC, as Polybius indicates (3.22). That few cities disappeared is a testimony to the success of the city-state models at containing tension and conflict, but also perhaps the solid agricultural basis for the economy of many Etruscan settlements. As the benefits from international trade diminished, new solutions had to be found and the archaeology reveals the social adjustments that had to be made. Each city-state went very much its own way, having brief collaborations and long-term trading connections, but with little sense that the 12- or 15-people confederations were more than symbolic institutions for ritual purposes.

This would prove to be a tragic failing. In the 4th century, several city-states seem to have started to revive their fortunes, concentrating on the renewed challenges from the Gauls and realizing the threat which Rome was beginning to pose. By then, however, Veii was already lost, and Rome's power was substantial. A huge concerted effort would be needed to defend the Etruscans' autonomy.

Chapter 8
Etruscan religion

The Etruscans were characterized in antiquity by their religious expertise. Livy called them the most religious of men, and in his own time, the haruspices, an order of priests with specific capacity to interpret signs in the entrails of sacrificed animals, held an important position in Roman religious life, and had done so for centuries. Here more than anywhere else we see the influence of Etruscan writings; they seem to have written down a great deal about their interpretative practices, and also about what happened after death. These books seem to have been much consulted, or at least the information within them was contextualized into Roman understandings of religion. Furthermore, in the place of the 'mysterious origins', a claim can be made for the mysteriousness of their religious practices, and in particular of the apparent fatalism of Etruscan religion; an attitude of gloomy submission to the irrevocable decisions of the gods. None of this quite describes the evidence however and we need to step back a little before arriving at such a grand conclusion.

Evidence of sanctuaries and temples shows lavish architectural expenditure from the later 6th century. Inscriptions indicate the quite formulaic and rule-bound nature of the worship; and we have more information from Latin authors on this subject than we do on most aspects of Etruscan life. However, two highly significant forms of evidence are also ones which are peculiarly Etruscan: the evidence from burials, both the sarcophagi themselves, and also the tomb paintings which decorate some surviving tombs; and mirrors. Made of bronze, one surface was highly polished to permit some reflection, and the other carefully inscribed with figures and scenes, often with the names of the actors. They may have been a common wedding gift. It is perhaps insufficiently emphasized that the grand state religion with its temples and priests, and the familial contexts of burials and boudoirs—if that was the right place for mirrors—may have reflected rather different kinds of religion. Our desperation for evidence makes us try to construct something called Etruscan religion, but that may cover many different experiences spread amongst different cities, classes, genders, and individuals.

That said, the funeral does seem to have been a focus for much expression of what one might call religious behaviour and thought. There are suggestions that in the 8th century, Villanovan culture had banquets alongside funerals. Representations of animals are frequent in funerary contexts, and some at least overtly reflect themes of fecundity and procreations—bulls and deer for instance. Sex, which tends to be somewhat obscured in later Etruscan art, is more apparent.

Whether the Etruscans imagined their deities as in human form at this stage is doubtful. Indeed, perhaps the prior question is what sort of deities the Etruscans had; we are familiar with classical gods being highly mythologized, their relations with each other, and indeed with humans, being characterized by all too recognizable human emotions. The early Etruscans may have been much more interested in phenomena. The chief god of the Etruscans, Tinia, is a god of lightning.

To an extent—but only to an extent—the Greeks changed all that. The complex genealogy and mythology through which the

Greeks constructed a religious world, and represented it in storytelling and vase painting and other sorts of media, had an undoubted impact on the way the Etruscans thought about their own gods from the 7th century at least. Not only do we find figures like Herkle and Aplu (Hercules and Apollo); we also find local mythological representations from the 6th century, and probably local myth-making too. Without necessarily losing the specificities of their own religion, the Etruscans seem to have found aspects of the Greek mythological world appropriate to their own, and anthropomorphism was one. Another critically important Greek introduction may have been the elaborate paraphernalia of sacrifice, which will have had consequences for the physical appearance and structure of cult places.

One intriguing aspect does deserve mention, and that is the persistent indeterminacy of Etruscan deities, something which may reflect their earlier nature. Some of them have both a male and a female version. Mirrors show Maris as a baby—but sometimes as one, two, or three babies. How they differed from each other is unclear. According to Roman sources, the Di Involuti or the Shrouded Gods were sufficiently powerful that even Tinia had to ask their permission, but they are otherwise utterly mysterious. The Di Consentes, 12 counselling gods, were equally vague, although the Romans systematized them, and the emperor Julian built a portico to them in the 4th century AD. The Aiser may be another collective term; we know this is a word used for god because after Julius Caesar's death an inscription naming him was struck by lightning, removing the letter *c*, and leaving a word close enough to the Etruscan for a god. The gods are regularly seen in counsel, and together, in Etruscan art. A picture of the Etruscans as a people who, in imitation of the way they perceived their deities, spent a lot of time talking to each other would be utterly consistent with the accounts of the 12 peoples who allegedly met at Fanum Voltumnae but hardly ever seem to have decided anything.

This level of indeterminacy however survives in some Roman deities (the Lares, Manes, and others) and perhaps in the abstract deities who seem to appear early in Roman religion (e.g. Robigo the deity of mildew) and the subsequent inventions such as Spes (Hope) and Salus (Safety), though one can see the Romans applying rules and logic. How did the Etruscans discover their own religion?

The Etruscans claimed that their religion had been revealed to them. A peasant was ploughing a field near Tarquinia and was astounded to see a child with the face of an old man arising from the furrow. He cried out, and all the people of Etruria came. Led by Tarchunus or Tarchon, a Tarquinian, they learnt the secrets of haruspicy, but also possibly the material in the Libri Acherontici about the nature of the underworld. The child, who was called Tages, then disappeared. Various versions existed of this story, but the essentials remained the same, and the discovery of a deep hole and the burial of a child who may have been epileptic near the Ara della Regina in Tarquinia in the later 9th century has made for some intriguing possibilities.

There are other prophetic figures too; Vegoia from Chiusi revealed the secrets of thunderbolts, the laws surrounding property, and also hinted at the social unrest that would come when slaves or masters disregarded them. Chalchas, a seer in Homer, also appears on Etruscan mirrors; and so does a disembodied head. Although the Tages myth was the one which survived best (John Lydus, a 6th century AD Byzantine writer, was using something he thought was Tarchon's book of questions to Tages, and an African priest, Longinianus, told St Augustine in the 5th century that he put Tages on the same level as Orpheus and Hermes Trismegistus), other cities may have had their own sources of inspiration. As a whole, the Etruscans seem to have developed a sense of their own ultimate demise; their theory of *saecula* or centuries tends towards a moment of doom at the end of the tenth. This may be a prophecy after the event—after the Roman conquest when it was clear that there was a limit to Etruscan autonomy.

These stories of the revelation of Etruscan religion provided the justification for the construction of a body of technical literature on various phenomena. We know a little about Etruscan views on thunderbolts because they were discussed by Seneca the Elder in the 1st century AD, who noted that the key difference was that most people thought that thunder and lightning came because clouds had gathered, but the Etruscans thought that clouds gathered in order to create thunder and lightning. The first task was to identify and understand, the second to interpret, and the third to expiate. We have a lengthy account of what lightning may entail—the so-called brontoscopic calendar of Nigidius Figulus from the 1st century BC. Many of the events portended are of political unrest, another indication of Etruscan concern with the unruliness of their communities. Kings could summon lightning—Numa and Lars Porsenna did so successfully, Tullus Hostilius managed to summon it onto his own palace and kill himself. This seems to have remained an Etruscan speciality; when Alaric led his Visigoths against Rome in the 5th century AD, the Pope forbade a group of haruspices from trying to summon lightning onto the enemy.

It was not only lightning which had such predictive power. The flight of birds, observed by augurs, was very important at Rome. Without the favourable interpretation of the auspices, no public act could be begun, no power assumed. Similar practices may have existed in Etruria; in the François Tomb at Vulci, Vel Saties observes the behaviour of a woodpecker. Critically, the whole art of auspices depended on the division of the visible space into quarters—which quarter the birds appeared in was critical. The same was true for lightning, and so there had to be a point from which one observed and an organization of space. Onto this organization the gods could be mapped to give a more accurate determination of the area which would be affected.

We have the best idea of this from Martianus Capella, who wrote in the 5th century AD in Roman Africa. Although there is a lot of later interpretation and systematization going on here, his complicated arrangement of space and divine attributes rings true of a religion which was strongly driven by the desire to predict and understand.

The most well-known aspect of this is the Etruscan specialism of haruspicy, divination by the observation of sheep's liver. Sacrifice is an absolutely central part of most ancient Mediterranean religious practice. A great deal has been written about humanity's recurring belief that by the death of another creature (sometimes another human) wisdom or force can be gained. The scapegoat, the alleged power of the blood of another creature, the complex social binding created by the ritual eating of the animal after sacrifice and after the gods have had their share, all this and much more surround the act of sacrifice. The Etruscan concentration on sheeps' livers can be seen in the famous bronze model of a liver from Piacenza, made perhaps in the 3rd or 2nd century BC, which has inscribed upon it the names of various deities (Figure 13). As with Martianus Capella's picture of the cosmos, so here we see a concern with division and attribution. The presence or absence of blemishes, malformations, and colour all hinted at divine intentions.

The haruspices comprised an order of 60 experts; an inscribed list from the early 1st century AD of their leading members going back some centuries was found at Tarquinia. As one might expect, to have such knowledge was not given to all; it appears to have been a highly elite order. There are indications that the south Etruscan elite supported Pompey against Caesar in the civil wars, and it is interesting that Caesar, who, whatever his own beliefs, was respectful of Roman religion on the whole, persistently ignored the haruspices, including allegedly the famous last one about the Ides of March in 44 BC, passed on by the chief haruspex, possibly a Spurinna from Tarquinia.

13. The most famous symbol of Etruscan religion, this bronze model of a liver from the second half of the 2nd century BC is about 12 cm in length, and is more or less the same as a real sheep's liver, with a stylized caudate lobe and gall-bladder. The model is covered with the names of Etruscan deities, and around the outside has the 16 divisions of the Etruscan view of the sky, and it is reasonably certain that this is some form of instruction manual for haruspicy

Tarquinia also provides an excellent idea of how a haruspex represented himself on the late 3rd century sarcophagus of Laris Pulenas (Figure 14). He reclines on his bed with an unrolled text—possibly intended to represent one of the linen books for which Etruria was well known. An inscription, nine lines in extent, states: 'Laris Pulenas, son of Larce, grandson of Larth, grandson of Velthur, great grandson of Pule Laris Creice...he wrote this book of haruspicy.' He was a magistrate too, and served the cult of Catha (Bacchus?) and Hermes, and Culsl, the god of the door, who was similar, it appears, to Janus. Here we see precisely the kind of mix of political office and religious function that we see in Rome. This is all part of the same world of privilege and duty, of expertise and inheritance. Even, or rather, especially in death, the Etruscan elite paraded their life's achievements. It is possible that the increasingly written and

14. 2 m by 0.62 m × 0.63 m, this sarcophagus from around 200 BC comes from Tarquinia and shows Laris Pulenas with his inscription. Below, winged figures and figures with hammers can be seen, who are often visible accompanying the deceased into the underworld

perhaps specialized Etruscan ritual may have assisted a hierarchical political system to sustain a relatively conservative social order, one which aided Etruscan recovery after the crisis of the 5th century, but also was exploited by the Romans in the 4th century and beyond.

The relationship between Etruscan beliefs about the gods and their beliefs about the afterlife is not wholly clear. We do not hear of any direct correlation between one's behaviour in the one sphere and the results in the other; we do not know of any kind of 'hell', though other contemporary societies philosophized about the rewards of virtue. Although some deities and demons have some role below, including Tinia, it is not clear that after death humans attained a closer relationship to the gods. They are ushered by the gods or demons into another world, but little has survived to help us understand that world. The Libri Acherontici or books of the Underworld may have had much more to say, and at least one possibility is that they were heavily spatial in concern, in other words, they worked out some kind of topography to help guide the lost soul.

However, from the beginning, it is in a funerary context that we come closest to some of the most direct expressions of ritual behaviour, and hints at personal belief systems. The Etruscans seem to have seen the progress to another life or another world as a journey—a procession such as accompanied so much of their civic life. A number of tombs from the later 6th and early 5th centuries have doors painted at the back; and in later paintings we see depictions of admittedly terrifying looking figures like Charun and Vanth who seem to be escorting the soul, often across water. These images have to be read against images of monsters and exotic animals on the one hand, and beautiful images of fertility, dance, and life on the other. Whatever the Etruscan view of death, they seemed determined to enjoy life, and perhaps hoped that notwithstanding the terrors of death, the joys could be replicated once the journey had passed. Was Charun there to terrify the dead soul or to scare off other monsters?

The funeral seems to have involved family celebrations which probably included feasting somewhere—perhaps in the vicinity of the tomb. Food deposits seem to have been left in some instances, but they were perhaps more intended for the sustenance of the deceased. It certainly appears that the Etruscans enjoyed games at funerals, and these were often highly dangerous, and might themselves lead to death. The Etruscans were said to have invented gladiatorial games, and specialized in boxing, which in antiquity was stomach-churningly brutal. Metal could be inserted into the leather thongs the boxers wrapped around their fists. Games on horseback or running alongside horses, or chariot races were all fraught with danger. Perhaps the Etruscans felt that such bloodshed animated or assisted the soul's passage; but we have to accept that they may simply have had a taste for it.

Somewhere into this we need to fit an apparently strong attachment to one's ancestors. Many Etruscan tombs reflect relatively large groups. Whether these be dug into natural cliffs as at Norchia, dug down into the tufa as at Tarquinia, or constructed under huge mounds as at Cerveteri, the arrangement of dynasties of burials, coupled with early evidence of statues in or just outside tombs, and those long genealogical inscriptions like that of Laris Pulenas, tend to suggest that the Etruscans valued familial solidarity.

The tombs themselves represented substantial investments, as did some of the highly wrought sarcophagi we see, such as the sarcophagus of the married couple ('Sarcofago degli sposi') from the 6th century, or the alabaster sarcophagi from Volterra. Later examples can have very highly wrought decoration, often with mythical scenes of death and disaster on the sarcophagi; the fratricidal strife underlying the Greek myth of the Seven against Thebes is a particularly good and common example. We cannot say for sure how the Etruscans reconciled their commemoration of the deceased and a picture of violent death; it may be that they thus put the deceased into association with the world of the hero, or it may be that it was a statement of culture, an indication of one's ability to appreciate the world of epic and theatre. This raises considerable and difficult questions about what the Etruscans took from Greek myth; whilst we have seen that some deities are incorporated or assimilated, and it is hard to see how Hercules was thought of without his labours, nevertheless, the Etruscans may have seen Greek myth as a reinforcement of their own pantheon, and an entertaining presentation of quasi-historical morality tales.

Tomb paintings are one of the most striking enhancements of the interior space of the tomb. Painting can include decoration of roofs, but is far from ubiquitous. One famous tomb represents ordinary objects—and indeed domestic animals—in relief, and many are plain. Tomb painting has now been found in a very early tomb at Veii, from the early seventh century, and that suggests it was a strong local practice since all the parallels that are adduced, for instance from Macedonian tombs, or from Paestum in the south, are later. Some scenes are mythical, but many are representations of dancing, feasting, and drinking. The diversity is striking; looking through a catalogue of Etruscan tomb painting, one is struck rather by a variety that presumably derived from personal taste. The same is true of the remarkable site of Norchia high above a river valley; each tomb is cut into the rock face, and then decorated with pediments and other architectural details.

Visitors to Etruscan sites are therefore often readily persuaded that the most significant feature of Etruscan belief relates to theories of the afterlife. This feeds into a view, often expressed, about the fatalism of the Etruscans. Obsessed with death, pursuing all sorts of recondite and bloody inspections to discern the future, and believing, it would seem, in a theory of their own demise, the Etruscans might be assumed to have been rather gloomy. Their adoption of a degree of unflinching realism in portraiture can lend weight to this; on later sarcophagi, the depiction of the beautiful man or woman has given way, and Etruscans often look old and solemn. Yet we need to keep this view in balance.

Etruscans have been found in the 1st century BC in Tunisia and in Egypt, yet still following their long-established rituals. It was precisely in this context that someone wrote down a long ritual calendar, using the traditional Etruscan medium of a linen book, and that would in time become the wrapping for a very un-Etruscan mummy. Whilst ritual can be seen as an unenlightened grasping after certainty, it is interesting to reflect on how comprehensible the Etruscans seem to have felt the world to be. As the individual deities crystallized out of a perhaps more diffuse, non-anthropomorphic world of forces and influences, the Etruscans harnessed them to a science of observation in a way that exceeded anything the Greeks had done. This science was admired and adopted. It was sustained and it was self-confident. To argue for several centuries in highly concrete ways about the gods' demonstration of their will towards humanity in the behaviour of birds, the nature of thunderbolts, and the marks on the livers of sheep suggests a view that the world makes some kind of sense, all other indications to the contrary. If an Etruscan went to his or her end with a robustly reinforced knowledge of what would happen next, and that its horrors were merely those of transition, he or she perhaps had less cause for gloom. In that way, Tages could be portrayed as a psychopomp (a leader of souls) exactly like Hermes Trismegistus and Orpheus, conveying a sense of certainty through teaching which gained authority through its obscurity. Laris Pulenas may look serious, but he was also perhaps seriously certain.

Chapter 9
The Roman conquest

The 5th century saw Etruria lose much of its sway in the western Mediterranean in the face of stiff competition from the Greeks of Campania, and others. Disruptions to burial practices and the disappearance of some family names hint at a broader social revolution behind this loss. Those Etruscans who had relied perhaps on their overseas markets had to find new sources of revenue, or build up the more traditional agricultural base. The brontoscopic calendar we referred to in the previous chapter, whilst it may well have very old roots indeed, perhaps even in Mesopotamia, and is a Latin copy of the Etruscan original, which we cannot date, refers constantly to the threats of disease, drought, rain, and frost to crops, cattle, birds, fish—and the oscillation in human fortune between scarcity and plenty. The mineral, agricultural, and marine resources may have been enough to keep some Etruscans prosperous, once the labour force, perhaps not wholly Etruscan, had been organized (and even Etruscan slaves were said to be well fed). These also made it an attractive region for the Romans.

The Roman conquest of Etruria was only part of their much broader drive to domination. It is part of their expansion within Italy which was largely complete in a military sense by the end of the 3rd century BC; the spread of a cultural package including Latin continued for another 200 years or so. Different regions of

Italy experienced this cultural revolution in different ways, but when Augustus evoked the concept of *tota Italia*, all Italy, late in the 1st century BC, he was to some extent expressing a capacity to take the whole of the peninsula as a single entity, albeit divided into regions.

We are quite well informed about this process; there are many questions, but we have a basic narrative. On the other hand, the absence of local information and different versions from the Roman one leaves a terrible gap. One way of thinking about this is to look at how an Etruscan reflected on his past from the vantage point of the 1st century AD. In the early imperial period, in the forum at Tarquinia, at least three inscriptions on marble were set up as statue bases in honour of the family of the Spurinna, attested at Tarquinia from the 6th century BC. One relates how Velthur Spurinna, son of Larth, led a contingent into battle in Sicily. Thucydides refers to a small Etruscan contingent of three pentekonters (50-oared ships) in 414/13 BC in the siege of Syracuse, but there may have been another context. Another refers to a king Orgulnius at Cerveteri who was either expelled or restored by Aulus Spurinna, who also put down a slave revolt at Arretium and captured nine Latin cities and perhaps operated also in the Faliscan region. This may be a reference not to the 6th century, when the Etruscans and the Romans were on equal terms, but is a claim for an Etruscan victory in a subsequent period when the Roman sources tend to claim supremacy. In any case, the inscriptions show that local historical tradition did survive. The other major inscription in the forum was a chronological list of haruspices. It is entirely possible that the Etruscans kept lists of magistrates and their actions, just as the Romans did in their Annales Maximi, preserved by the pontifices. Sadly, none has survived; and even this inscription, which may well reflect an Etruscan victory and a moment of local civic pride, was written in Latin.

These inscriptions can stand for the complexities of this period. One narrative is of Roman military success; another of the disappearance of local culture; but a third is the reinterpretation of that culture within the context of Roman power. The Etruscans had to navigate and negotiate their undeniable loss of authority and autonomy, and the story was inevitably more nuanced than we can recover.

The conflict with Veii, and the conquest of the city in 396 BC, was deeply rooted in Rome's conception of herself. Coming as it did just before the sack of Rome by the Gauls in 390 BC, it was part of a narrative of success, disaster, and recovery which was all pinned on the great Roman hero Camillus, who won at Veii, fell from grace, and then returned to rescue Rome. It is very important to note that, for all the uncertainties, there can be no doubt that Veii did indeed fall to Rome in the early 4th century, and the city was destroyed. In fact, one of the reasons why we do have relatively good evidence for aspects of archaic Veii is because the city was demolished and ritually buried.

Much of the narrative of the contest is unreliable. The ten-year siege alleged by some of the sources is a bad parody of the Trojan War. Many of the stories of prodigies which attended the Roman victory are equally likely to be colouring after the event. Yet the prize was clear, and the consequences very visible. Whoever won would have control of the lower reaches of the Tiber to the sea. Veii seems to have hung on, but after defeat, Ostia becomes a Roman colonial settlement; that gave Rome control of the salt-pans at the mouth of the Tiber, which will have been an important resource for meat preservation amongst other things, and also control of the Grotta Oscura tufa which came from the territory of Veii. This distinctively coloured limestone can be seen in some of the 4th century stretches of Rome's defensive circumvallation wall, and notably the long section surviving near Termini station.

Three other aspects of this highly notable success need to be mentioned. First, the conquest of Veii was also associated with a very powerful act of religious appropriation. The goddess Juno was invited to leave the ruined city, and is said to have assented through her statue nodding, and the cult was brought to Rome. This act of evocation was rare, and for that reason alone the tradition may be reliable. It is possible that here we see another aspect of the tremendous effort by the Romans to eradicate Veii.

Second, the territory itself was distributed to Romans for agricultural purposes. Land redistribution would become a contentious and long-standing theme of Roman Republican history. It may indicate however a reason why the whole relationship with Veii was so fraught. This was no normal boundary dispute, but a war for survival. It is interesting that the other Etruscans stood to one side, as far as we can tell, alleging Veii's impiety. Was Veii's unpopularity due to her expansion into the Faliscan area, and control of the lower reaches of the Tiber? Veii fought independently, and after her defeat was unavailable to act alone or in consort with others.

Third, Veii was an extremely important city in the context of the Faliscan people, a distinct group who occupied a small corner of the territory between the sea and the Tiber river. It has often been thought that Veii was probably their leading city in reality, although the Faliscans have their own distinctive cultural aspects. Intriguingly, the Faliscan region picks up after the fall of Veii, with a strong ceramic production, which might suggest that the domination by Veii was repressive. However, it was an edgy time since the defeat of Veii also left the Faliscans directly exposed to the Romans, and the Roman colonies of Sutri and Nepi were founded in 383 BC.

Understanding Roman imperial expansion in the 4th century is not straightforward. We have more detailed information about magistrates, battles, and triumphs, but Roman writers were guilty of exaggeration and error. Yet Rome's progress was steady and probably methodical. To what extent was Rome aggressively pursuing a premeditated campaign of conquest; would it be fair for instance to ask the question at what point did the Romans decide to conquer Etruria; or indeed to expect to be able to give an answer? On the one hand, the Romans prized military victory, extolled those who achieved it, and used the proceeds to develop their city and to gain fortunes. Annual campaigning seems to have been a way of life for many central Italian city states. Although the Romans developed a highly sophisticated rhetoric and ritual to represent themselves always as the aggrieved party in any war, in truth, the habit of conflict was deep-seated. Maintaining a strong and visibly successful army was an important part of Roman power, and during a turbulent period in the 5th century, when all the Latins were forced to cooperate against various threats, Rome had grown larger and stronger. This led to challenges from the allied Latins in the early 4th century, which they lost.

The debate over just how aggressive the Romans were goes all the way back to antiquity. It would be overstated to assume that Rome had in mind a pan-Italian empire when she conquered and sacked Veii, but it does seem that Rome was always conscious of the next step. The Faliscan colonies seem to support such a view; recognizing that Veii was so significant in the Faliscan region, Rome moved rapidly to secure that position. Equally, it is interesting to see how significant for the Romans was the progress along the Tiber river. Control of the most significant natural barrier but also a vital communication link permitted a degree of security and closed the Etruscans off from one vital territorial advantage.

Did the Etruscans begin to appreciate the potential danger they were in? We are told that in 353 Falerii, Tarquinia, and Cerveteri united against the Romans, and Livy says the whole of Etruria took part. The outcome was a series of arrangements of one kind or another with the various parties. For much of this period Rome was in some difficulties—there was a Gallic incursion, a Latin revolt, and a major campaign against the Samnites in which there were two crushing defeats for the Romans at the Caudine Forks and Lautulae. Why did the Etruscans not combine regularly and determinedly against the Romans?

Part of the answer may be the complex Etruscan federal structure. We know that the Etruscans had a shared sanctuary at Fanum Voltumnae, and one of the major discoveries of recent years has been the identification of what seems to have been the site, outside Orvieto (ancient Volsinii) at Campo della Fiera. Monumental roads, remains of large temples, fountains, a huge collection of Greek ceramics and evidence of continued activity right through the Roman period, including a substantial bath building, all attest to a site of the greatest importance.

The meetings of the Etruscan peoples at Fanum Voltumnae may have offered an opportunity for the discussion of concerted action, but we know nothing about how these worked, and for the northern cities, Rome may have seemed a long way away, and the Gallic threat more immediate and unnerving. So it was for the southern cities to take the lead, and yet there is a question about what they had to gain? Territorially, the Etruscan cities were relatively well placed. If our previous analysis of Etruscan expansionism is correct, territorial conquest and acquisition was not an Etruscan practice. Rome's habit of absorbing conquered peoples into her citizenship, and thereby augmenting her population, may have had consequences for Roman demography and the Roman army which were not paralleled in Etruscan cities. There may have been more sporadic violence and conflict than we see, but for the most part the conquest of Veii, the Faliscan colonies, and a brief spat in the middle of the 4th century seem the limit of Roman capacity whilst their other campaigns were pressing.

Late in the 4th century, the narrative changes. From 311 to 308 the sources give a confusing sequence of campaigns and battles around Sutrium, in Umbria and as far north as the Ciminus forest (described as a terrifyingly dense place by Livy, who exaggerated). One way of understanding the campaigns is to see them again as a steady progress up the Tiber river, with engagements from there into Etruria. It is not easy to see a concerted effort of coalition by the Etruscans, or a single approach to the areas in which the Romans had campaigned. Colonies are founded closer to the Tiber, but further into Etruria we find vague agreements between Rome and the Etruscan cities.

There is no reason to think that the peace was thought to be permanent on either side. By the late 4th century, Rome had geared itself up to a cycle of warfare that at some level already seems obsessive, but her major foe, the Samnites, was behaving similarly. The repetitive and at times highly ritualized form of this warfare is noteworthy. Both sides were in some senses expressing their values of valour and manliness as much as they were achieving real gains. For the Samnites, the key issue must have been independence and access to the lowland plains. For the Romans, territorial advantage and deep defences may have been part of it, but there is rapacity here too. The Etruscans, interestingly, are caught up into this conflict, and at a time when they are also in some cases trying to resolve substantial internal difficulties. What the Roman conquest of Etruria shows up most clearly, and for almost the first time with such definition, is the social structure of the Etruscan towns.

The battle which the sources focus on is a massive set piece at Sentinum in 295 BC in which the Samnites converge with the Etruscans and the Umbrians, and the Gauls join in too. The battle of Sentinum was, like many of the set pieces of the middle Republic, heavily worked up by the sources into a great Roman victory, but instead of bringing things to an end, we find everything starting again the following year. However the combination of forces reveals the complexity of the central Italian situation, with the Gauls now a real factor, and may betray a growing sense that the Romans were not going to stop. Throughout the first half of the 3rd century there were rumbling campaigns, complicated by the incursions of Gauls which now seem directed against the Etruscan cities. Cerveteri rebelled against Rome in the 270s and Volsinii in the 260s but by then resistance had largely come to an end.

One reason why resistance lasted as long as it did was the impregnability of Etruscan towns. Rosellae is the only one which fell completely to Rome after Veii. The others were too well situated. However there was also no need to sack them because the damage could be done elsewhere, in the territory. The combination of Gallic raids and Roman depredations was taking its toll. Whatever could be gained from commerce, agricultural wealth remained core to many and perhaps most Etruscan settlements, and what characterized the development of the great Etruscan cities was precisely their control of territory. The apparently relatively well-marked divisions, the sense of territory and frontier which may have arisen in the Villanovan revolution and seems clear through the period of Etruscan flourishing, depended on strong agriculture.

It is interesting therefore that one of our sources, Dionysius of Halicarnassus, speaks of the division in Etruria between the most powerful men, and the *penestai*, a word which in other contexts indicates something akin to serfdom, and a hint of arrogant treatment, in comparison with the more generous way the Romans treated their clients. We also know that there are a number of inscriptions to individuals who are characterized as *lautni*, which in a couple of valuable bilingual inscriptions is equated with *libertus* or freed man.

This is fairly tenuous evidence on which to hang an entire theory, but one hears of a number of occasions on which the Romans intervene on the side of Etruscan aristocrats who were in difficulty because of social strife. It happened at Arretium in 302, at Troilum in 293, and at Volsinii in 265–264, where the aristocrats had been expelled.

The Volsinii story is particularly highly wrought. The lower classes had been admitted to the army after repeated reverses in action against the Romans. They quickly rose in power, even reaching the local senate. The aristocrats appealed to the Romans (and were executed for their treachery) but the Romans seized the advantage, and attacked. Their victory in 264 BC led to the first gladiatorial games at Rome, and 2,000 bronze statues were taken from the town—it is likely that many came from the Fanum Voltumnae site. They restored the exiles—but in a new, less well-defended city. Cunningly, therefore the Romans had both supported the aristocrats and ruined the city's future chances of resisting Rome.

At Volsinii, it is hard to say who is less attractive: the duplicitous elite or the aggressive and stupid poor—and that of course is the point. The Romans have some bad times, but it is a long, slow, and ultimately successful process of amalgamation and compromise. The Volsinians do everything in a rush, act unspeakably, and bring ruin on themselves. An outsider might well have looked at Rome and seen its travails in similar sorts of ways, and that the Volsinians were divided, and other Etruscan cities too, seems probable. Knowing the way that Etruscan society operated, Romans regularly chose to back the elite; and in that way, they created a bond which permitted others to do all the hard work of maintaining peace and security. The apparent prosperity of a site like Tarquinia or Chiusi with its thriving hinterland before and indeed for a while after Roman conquest is indicative, although the destruction of Gravisca and the restructuring of the sacred areas of Pyrgi tell another story.

The Romans' major intervention was through confiscation of territory from the Etruscans. When Veii was destroyed, the territory confiscated was about 600 km²; in 281, a large amount of land was used for the colonies at Cosa, Alsium, Pyrgi, Saturnia, Gravisca, and Heba. Some of the land of Arretium might have been taken in 200 BC. We do not know how the Etruscans managed this loss. They may have integrated with the colonies (even if they resented their presence); they may have continued to farm confiscated land as later events imply.

There is a mixture then of some direct control, some symbolic strong arming, and some 'divide and rule' behaviour. Not only does this have the virtue of looking rather like other instances of Roman control, it also fits both the archaeological and epigraphic evidence of long-term continuity of elite families in the 3rd and 2nd centuries BC, and explains behaviour through that period. Neither in 225 BC when the Gauls mounted a very significant invasion, nor in the second Punic War when the Carthaginian general Hannibal had invaded Italy and came as close as anyone to destroying Rome, was there a generalized uprising by the Etruscans.

The resistance during the Hannibalic war is significant because again the Etruscans were not in an easy position. Hannibal seems to have made himself unpopular by his habit of raiding and pillaging to support his army, but one of Rome's two great defeats, at Lake Trasimene, happened in Etruria; they could scarcely have been unaware of how close to disaster Rome had come. Polybius suggests that Hannibal struggled to get access to the sea, which may imply that coastal Etruria had not been easy for him to get to, and only the Etruscans can have delivered that.

As the war went on, disaffection grew throughout Rome's allies, but also amongst Hannibal's. Both sides were making huge demands in terms of grain and other supplies, as well as manpower, which was being directed to distant fields of battle. Even when Hasdrubal entered Etruria, in 209–207, Rome had just two legions stationed there, and although there were fears of revolution it did not happen. Arretium, which had been one of the cities where the possibility of internal strife had been mooted a century before, is the city which seems to have most roused fears. In the jittery days of war though, overreaction and rumour were to be expected. Had the Roman presence in Etruria been universally hated, surely the Etruscans would have contributed more to Hannibal's campaign. That they did not shows perhaps that they realized that their own trading interests were not helped by a Carthaginian dominance in the western Mediterranean, perhaps that Hannibal and Hasdrubal signally failed to do their diplomacy well, but also that there was by the later 3rd century BC already a clear sense of a common interest at least between some Etruscan leaders and Rome. In terms of their contribution, in 225 BC, the Sabines and Etruscans provided 4,000 cavalry and 50,000 infantry against the Gauls, and the Umbrians 20,000 infantry; in 205 BC, when Scipio set about raising a fleet to finish the war, Cerveteri offered grain and supplies, Populonia iron, Tarquinia linen for the sails, Volterra grain and fittings, Arretium an extraordinary amount of armour and weaponry, and money, and Perugia, Chiusi, and Roselle wood for ships and grain. We do know that one man from Tarquinia, Larth Felsnas, fought for Hannibal and said so in his funerary inscription; many others must have fought with Rome.

In conclusion, the Hannibalic war shows that many Etruscans had cause to fight alongside Rome and not to rebel. Yet only a few years before, Cerveteri had been in rebellion. The most obvious way to understand this is to see Etruscan cities as divided (as Greek cities were) about the Romans. If the Romans steadfastly supported the aristocrats in cities where others were seeking and in some instances successfully gaining power, then it is unsurprising that there could be political doubts. The edginess of the times, and the Roman nervousness, probably came from that. Yet even after the Hannibalic war, when Rome might have decided that those moments of uncertainty deserved to be punished, it was the exception rather than the rule for the Romans to found colonies. They continued instead to trust their system of alliance.

There are exceptions; there are colonies at Cosa (273) on the coast—a strategically significant site. When Cerveteri revolted, it lost half its territory, and the likely colonies are Alsium, Fregenae, Castrum Novum, and Pyrgi. Luca and Luna were rather on the edges; Saturnia, Parma, and Mutina were again towards the further edges and perhaps looked north not south. It is also true that colonies were not just about controlling territory; they could also be used in the game of political reward. One way of benefiting one's followers as a Roman politician was to deliver them land in a Roman colony, and it is not excluded that some of those who moved into a colony and benefited from it were themselves Etruscans.

By the early 2nd century BC, Roman control in Italy up to the Po Valley was extremely strong. With the exception of the rather peculiar event in 91–89 BC which is called the Social War, and a few isolated outbreaks of violence, which appear to have been caused by bad behaviour by an individual magistrate rather than systemic opposition, Italy was as far as we can tell fairly peaceful. During this period, Rome was increasingly successful outside Italy, building the empire on which her fortune rested. So the transformations inside Italy tended to be cultural to an extent, and for that reason have been attributed to an effort by the Romans to create a homogeneous culture, or an assimilation to Roman culture by non-Romans. These kinds of choices and actions fall under the general modern term 'Romanization'.

This may be a good example of a debate being created almost artificially by the use of a shorthand terminology. There is little reason to think that the Romans had a cultural policy, or that all Italians were simply waiting for a better cultural package to come along. Variability and patchiness must have been the predominant experience, and we should not forget either that the notion of what it was to be Roman was itself under profound change and pressure in the 2nd and 1st centuries BC. The impact of the conquest of Greece was a complete reshaping of modes of thought and speech, both through the adoption of some practices and the rejection of others, and often at the same time and sometimes inexplicably in the same person. Cato the Elder, who allegedly despised the Greeks, wrote in the language and was learned in the history. The processes by which the Italian peninsula including Rome changed over this period contained manifold individual choices (just like the one that Larth Felsnas made in backing Hannibal), and under the pressure of evidence of that kind, an overarching term like Romanization buckles and fails.

Nevertheless, there were Roman moves which necessarily impacted on lives and landscapes, and one of the most obvious was the way that Roman road building reoriented movement across the countryside. The Roman roads in Etruria formed a complex system which linked up the colonial foundations and disrupted centuries-old connections between coast and hinterland. The Via Clodia (begun in the 280s BC) ran to the west of Lake Bracciano and the colony of Saturnia was later established on it. The Via Aurelia (begun in 241 BC) ran parallel to the coast cutting across the communication between Pyrgi and Cerveteri and Gravisca and Tarquinia. The Via Cassia (154 BC) made access to troublesome Arretium easier. The Via Flaminia created a powerful link across Etruria, through Umbria and colonies like Narnia and the allied town of Ocriculum (modern Otricoli) and right across to the colony of Ariminum on the Adriatic coast, which is a reminder of the importance of that coastline to the Romans, just as it had been significant for the Etruscans. Its date has been placed in the 240s, in 220, or in the 140s BC. The most obvious consequence of Roman aggression within this context is the Via Amerina which was built to link to Falerii Novi, the town which replaced Falerii Veteres which had been razed to the ground. The less obvious consequence is the towns and settlements which may have been deliberately not connected:

Cerveteri, Tarquinia, Vulci, Telamon, Vetulonia, Populonia, Faesulae, and other smaller settlements. The roads did however encourage the growth of so-called *fora*, marketplaces which had an important if somewhat invisible role as stopping places, new nodes of encounter, and often a connection to new organizations of territory.

The archaeological evidence shows different responses in different cities. Some continued strongly, with independent traditions in funerary sculpture for instance. However, many Etruscan cities show a diminution of evidence from the cities themselves in the 3rd and 2nd centuries BC, although some increase in agricultural activity and villas late in the 2nd and particularly in the 1st century BC. The other major indicator of Roman cultural power is the adoption of the Latin language, but there is little evidence to suppose that this gets under way before the Social War and it is to that fascinating conflict to which we turn now.

It is not possible to dissociate the events of the Social War (so named because it involved the *socii* or allies of Rome) from the highly complex issues of landownership that were raised in the time of the Gracchi. Famously Tiberius Gracchus was said to have claimed that when he left for his province, he looked around him in southern Etruria and saw a contradiction: a landscape deserted, but all the workers were barbarian slaves. This prompted him on his return to seek the tribunate of 133 BC and implement land reform to get Romans back on the land, restore a degree of fairness, and encourage a workforce who could also be part of the army.

What the Gracchi did was to enforce certain rules of landownership which had long existed but which had not been applied. There was a legal limit to the amount of land which was declared public land of the Roman people and it could only be held by a Roman citizen. The likely impact of this was to cause some Etruscans to be forced off land which they thought was theirs. If Tiberius Gracchus was seeing anything real, it may have been the absence of Roman citizens in the fertile and successful countryside of Etruria. Whilst Rome struggled, the Etruscans appeared to have done all too well. The major consequence of Tiberius' intervention however was uncertainty. Lawsuits abounded and people complained. Some Etruscans had already gained Roman citizenship so may have been able to lobby directly. Ties of acquaintance and shared interests crossed over the barriers set by legal definitions. Knowing one might lose one's land and be forced to yield it to some ignorant Roman remained for a century a matter of huge anger and ultimately it was self-defeating. Many of the Romans who were settled did not know what to do and drifted back to the city of Rome. So the Gracchan intervention may have prompted one of the underlying causes of subsequent discontent.

The revolt which we call the Social War started in 91 BC in the east and south, in the Abruzzo, southern Campania, and Apulia. The explosion of violence may not have been wholly unexpected, but it does seem under-motivated. The key issues appear to have been the capacity of Italians to share equally in the economic benefits of the developing Roman empire; and concerns that continued grants of land by Romans to Romans would leave Italians without homes and livelihood.

What then did the allies want? Scholarship has tended to argue that the allies wanted either Roman citizenship—which they won and quite quickly—or independence, which they failed to get. Another possibility is that different groups wanted different things; and another again is that they wanted to beat the Romans and then work out the consequences. It is not clear if the Etruscans and Umbrians, who joined later, wanted the same thing as the others. The Roman response was to fight hard but simultaneously to concede the citizenship.

There was nothing simple about the Social War. It may not even have been well understood at the time, and it has the characteristics of an explosion of frustration. Italians won (at the cost of some degree of autonomy) centuries of peace, but they had also become part of the murky politics of Rome. Over the next 50 years, Italians would be dragged in again and again to wars between Roman generals and hard men, lured by the offer of gain, and tied by genuine loyalty, victims of marauding armies or of vicious reprisals. Despite their access to the vote, Italians could do little to change the direction of events.

It is difficult to identify the degree of damage done to Etruria by the Social War because it was so rapidly followed by other conflicts. At the time of the Social War, the two key figures were the relatively elderly Marius, who held more consulships than any other Roman in the Republic, and the somewhat younger and violent Sulla, who returned from wars in the east determined to take power for himself. Although Marius and Sulla battled it out further to the south less than a decade after the end of the Social War, the evidence of coin hoards (coins buried but not recovered, and therefore an index of disruption) shows that throughout the 70s and 60s, the Etruscan countryside was suffering. Sulla's massive expropriations of land in Etruria to reward his followers in the late 80s BC remained a problem for decades, because it turned into a political football with promises of restitution never being fully concluded. Caesar and Pompey largely conducted their warfare outside Italy, but this still had the result of placing huge recruitment demands on Italians. In 41–40, Lucius Antonius, Mark Antony's younger brother, was forced by Caesar's heir, Octavian, into a siege in the Umbrian town of Perugia. He surrendered but the town's inhabitants were massacred. Presumably some of the eight legions of men he had recruited came from this part of Italy. Octavian and Mark Antony competed for legionary soldiers, and the situation at sea was also problematic, with Sicily occupied by Sextus Pompeius (Pompey's son). This must have damaged trade and commerce. The civil war ended outside Italy at Actium. It is generally agreed that by that time, Italy was exhausted.

However, the travails of Etruria were not over. On top of distributions made by the triumvirs Antony, Octavian, and Lepidus, between Actium and 13 BC, Octavian, who took the name Augustus, rewarded veterans with land. About 120,000 had been settled by 29 BC, and by the end of his reign, 300,000 veterans had received land or money. The land was largely distributed via colonies, and Etruria and Campania took the brunt. Some existing settlements were recolonized; some places may have had pre-existing viritane distribution of land which was overturned. The sequence at Veii for instance seems to see a Caesarian settlement with its own government, then removed by Augustus, who sends more settlers and then reinstates the government. In the end, the most visible evidence at Veii is a large villa and a bath complex. Colonies must have come with land organization; at Pisa (Colonia Obsequens Iulia Pisana; the names of Roman colonies left no doubt that things had changed) we see traces of the Augustan or triumviral centuriation. Only Tarquinia, Volsinii, and Clusium show no sign of intervention. No inscription in Etruscan is known after the reign of Augustus.

Chapter 10
Clothing and the Etruscan body

What did the Etruscans actually look like? The Etruscans were probably a little shorter than modern Italians. Heights between about 1.5 and 1.7 m (five foot two to six) would be around normal. In youth we would expect Etruscan males to be fit; but in later life they seem to have tended to fatness; funeral depictions show them carrying weight and this seems to be a sign of having lived well. Etruscans are known for an interest in boxing, which was a sport which favoured larger bodies; in Aristotle, we hear that boxers tend to have bigger diets than runners.

Modern scholarship does not take the body for granted. Anthropological studies have shown us that corporeality needs to be brought into our historical and anthropological studies. Bodily routines, experiences, and permissible behaviours are critical elements of human life; moreover, the way we look at bodies and present our own bodies is highly culturally constructed.

Nudity was not natural to the Etruscans, even in exercise, and this marks them out distinctly from the Greeks. Men tended at the very least to wear short pants or loincloths, often with heavy belts. Women wore robes, of linen. Over that, both sexes wore mantles in wool, fastened with fibulae on the right shoulder. Shoes were a particular Etruscan speciality; hinged sandals of wood and bronze survive archaeologically; even Athenian ladies allegedly sought after Etruscan shoes with gold laces; whilst a central European princess was buried with her repoussé gold plate shoes from Etruria. Ionian fashions in clothes and shoes can be detected, but Etruscan hats and hairstyles develop independently. Here, as perhaps nowhere else, we see the huge degree of cultural mimesis which existed in the Mediterranean. Etruscans and Greeks and others knew the latest fashions and chose which to follow (Figure 15). Cosmetics and hairstyle were especially prone to change and to attention. The apparently

15. This gold stud, 3 cm by 3.5 cm, was found in a tomb at Vignanello, near Viterbo, and dates to around 480 BC. In the centre, a reclining satyr, bearded and hairy, is surrounded by fine granulation with a flower decoration above and two volutes below. The piece shows the extraordinary skill of Etruscan gold work

careless locks of young men in mirrors and paintings were as artful as those of fashion-conscious Italians today; the Etruscan body (male and female) was anointed with oil, perfumed, depilated, and carefully groomed. Even dental care can be found; some of the best dentures from antiquity are gold prostheses from Etruria, carefully moulded to bridge between existing teeth.

The Greek fashion of representing the body ideally and naked is more accepted in the 4th century BC in Etruria—but it is not clear that it took off in real life. Conversely, the Italians regularly showed nursing mothers, which was not a Greek subject. It may over-interpret the evidence to suggest that the Etruscans had a greater appreciation of the body in all its phases and guises, whereas the Greeks appreciated the body beautiful and ridiculed what they perceived as ugliness, but the Etruscans maintained realism in portraiture, which was never a strong Greek trend, although it heavily influenced Roman aesthetics. One should also not overlook the detailed votive deposits of parts of the body, and sometimes bodies opened up to show the internal organs. This may reflect the donor's illness meeting an artist's quasi-medical knowledge, learnt perhaps from the battlefield, or surgery, or from the transposition of the knowledge of the viscera of animals to humans. It also reflects a sense of the body as a relation of parts to the whole; and some consciousness perhaps of the various functions of the bodily parts that is proto-scientific.

The Etruscans made choices about how to represent themselves; particularly obvious is their happiness to portray deceased males as well fed, and sometimes fat. This highly visual depiction of access to good food and a minimal requirement to work to get it presents the body very differently from the honed muscular youth of Greek sculpture, or the unkempt philosopher, although both those stereotypes themselves depended on funded leisure. How bodies are represented and the attitudes to bodily behaviour are critical signposts to larger cultural issues.

Although the deep divide was between Greeks and barbarians, not all barbarians were the same. The otherness of the Etruscans was noted in antiquity, and one assumes was understood by the Etruscans.

The most famous description of the Etruscans as different relates specifically to bodily behaviour. Theopompus, a Greek historian writing in the 4th century BC, produced this marvellously prurient account:

> Sharing wives is an established Etruscan custom. Etruscan women take particular care of their bodies and exercise often, sometimes along with the men, and sometimes by themselves. It is not a disgrace for them to be seen naked. They do not share their couches with their husbands but with the other men who happen to be present, and they propose toasts to anyone they choose. They are expert drinkers and very attractive.
>
> The Etruscans raise all the children that are born, without knowing who their fathers are. The children live the way their parents live, often attending drinking parties and having sexual relations with all the women. It is no disgrace for them to do anything in the open, or to be seen having it done to them, for they consider it a native custom. So far from thinking it disgraceful, they say when someone asks to see the master of the house, and he is making love, that he is doing so-and-so, calling the indecent action by its name.
>
> When they are having sexual relations either with courtesans or within their family, they do as follows: after they have stopped drinking and are about to go to bed, while the lamps are still lit, servants bring in courtesans, or boys, or sometimes even their wives. And when they have enjoyed these they bring in boys, and make love to them. They sometimes make love and have intercourse while people are watching them, but most of the time they put screens woven of sticks around the beds, and throw cloths on top of them.
>
> They are keen on making love to women, but they particularly enjoy boys and youths. The youths in Etruria are very good-looking,

because they live in luxury and keep their bodies smooth. In fact all
the barbarians in the West use pitch to pull out and shave off the
hair on their bodies.

Rather more soberly, we are told that Aristotle remarked on how
the Etruscans dined with their wives, reclining with them under
the same blanket.

How much credence should we give to Theopompus' account?
Much of it is stereotypical inversions of appropriate Greek
behaviour. Some of it is highly reminiscent of philosophical
recommendations. So Plato recommended a loosening of the strict
rules over family; but the twist here is that it is the women
who seem to be getting the best of the deal, expertly drinking
and choosing their mates. As for preoccupation with descent,
if there is one thing we can derive from Etruscan tombs
and naming practices, it is that they were very concerned with
such matters.

If the Etruscans were forthright about their enjoyment of sex,
they can hardly have been more so than the Greeks as reflected
in Athenian comedy; Italian humour also seems to have
been highly robust. Tomb paintings do show men and women
and men and men engaged in sexual activity, but a taste for
male homosexuality does not mark out the Etruscans from
contemporary societies. As for hairiness, the barber shop was not
an Italian invention.

In the end, this famous and often quoted passage looks
increasingly like a piece of ethnographic fantasy. The note that
rings truest is Aristotle's account of the position of women
alongside men. Throughout Etruscan history, there are indications
of respect for women, of symbols of female authority, of their
literacy, both actual but also in terms of a capacity to use and
enjoy the highly allusive material of Etruscan myth. We know next
to nothing about the legal capacities of Etruscan women, and

issues such as ownership, but the regular representation of single women on sarcophagi may imply that a woman could construct a visibly independent life.

How ironic it is therefore, that the longest description of what the Etruscans were actually like in terms of behaviour and cultural activity may turn out to be largely worthless as an account of the Etruscans and only indicative of the extraordinary capacity of the Greeks to bend everything to a distorted reflection of their own cultural prejudices. Theopompus' point seems to be that the Etruscans are bad Greeks; their women are too out of control and

16. 1.83 m long, this highly painted sarcophagus came from a settlement near Chiusi and is dated to the first quarter of the 2nd century BC. On the walls of the small chamber tomb (which included only her sarcophagus) had hung silver objects, including a mirror, a scent bottle, a lidded box, and a strigil (used to scrape ointments from the skin). The box is formed from architectural motifs; and the name of the owners was inscribed in the clay at the bottom before firing. The lid is made in two parts; it shows the owner drawing back a veil; she holds a mirror, and is wearing a tiara, a necklace, a bracelet on her upper and lower arm, and earrings

their enjoyment of the same kinds of sex as the Greeks enjoyed was inappropriate in occasion and manner.

A last word might go to a couple of Etruscan women. Early in the 2nd century BC, Seianti Hanunia Tlesnasa had herself buried in a painted terracotta sarcophagus near Chiusi (Figure 16). She draws back a veil to reveal quite a full face, and she wears elegant jewellery on her ears and round her neck and arms. In reality, she died in her fifties, as analysis of her surviving skeleton has shown. She appears to have had a riding accident when young, and suffered from bad teeth and gum disease. Portraits may mislead therefore, but maybe Seianti Hanunia chose her youthful self as a statement of determination, of ongoing energy, of regret at a life left less mobile and comfortable.

Lastly, we know that Livia, Augustus' wife, had a friend called Urgulania, who felt herself so above the laws that she refused to attend court when summoned. One Orgolnius Velthume was king of Cerveteri, according to the Elogia Tarquiniensia, and so she came from a royal family, like Augustus' friend Maecenas. Her granddaughter was Claudius' first wife; and she married into a family, the Plautii Laterani, in whose house (under modern S. Giovanni in Laterano) a throne was found which in shape and decoration is deeply reminiscent of earlier Etruscan forms.

Chapter 11
Imperial epilogue

For many modern accounts of the Etruscans, their story is nearly at an end. Massive land redistributions, the transformation of the language from one natively spoken to one which was no more than the object of academic study, decline in the towns, and a generalized absence of funerary evidence leads one quickly to assume that to all intents and purposes, the Etruscans had disappeared. The last act in this sad story tends to be assigned to the emperor Claudius, whom we have already seen married to the descendant of Etruscan kings, and trying to make sense of Etruscan history. He wrote a 20-volume account of the Etruscans, of which nothing survives. This 'known unknown' is the single most frustrating and disappointing gap; even if Claudius had composed a hotch-potch of daft myths and mistaken historical reconstructions, he cannot have failed to include the kind of evidence we must now either glean from scraps, or simply confess we do not have. Yet there is no evidence that anyone read it even at the time.

With their language no longer spoken, no native literature, and a dismal aura of decline, there may seem little else to say about the Etruscans. Yet that would be a mistake. Understanding what happened in Etruria between the Augustan period and the fall of the Roman empire is key to understanding how (and how well) the empire worked, and the Etruscans were contributing to that story.

Take Faesulae (Fiesole); an important minor centre from the 9th century BC, it was turned into a Sullan colony and preceded the triumviral colony of Florentia (Florence), with which it would have close ties (Florence even contributed to the restoration of the Capitolium at Fiesole). The visitor will be guided into a well-presented area of archaeological remains—all Roman, with a restored complex of theatre, baths, and temple. Over 30 Latin inscriptions have been found. A. Faltennius and his third wife, Ladinnia, have characteristically Etruscan names but he identifies himself carefully with his Roman tribal affiliation (son of Gaius, of the Scaptian tribe, and holding the office of *sevir*). L. Tettius Probus and L. Tettius Maximus (impeccably Roman) lament a wife and mother. Lucius Crescens has a daughter called Tigris (not very Roman at all). C. Vettius Chrysogonus' family will have owed much to Sulla's henchman of the same name. Others were from servile origins: Eutychus, Hilarus, and Corinthus. It is the standard mix for a prosperous little town of a few thousand souls.

In 4 BC, when Augustus was consul with Lucius Sulla (descendant of the dictator and founder of the colony), one Gaius Crispinus Hilarius (a free man, though with that name not originally Roman) went up to the Capitol at Rome to sacrifice preceded by his 8 children, 27 grandchildren, 18 great grandchildren, and 8 granddaughters by marriage. We hear of guilds and the worshippers of Saturnus, and there is a dedication to Isis. Thereafter, we hear nothing until Stilicho defeats Radagaisus and the Vandals and Suevi in 406, and the town has a difficult time in the 6th century Gothic Wars. It recovered its independence and Fra Angelico lived there in a convent. Several families—amongst them the Medici—created beautiful Renaissance villas on the slopes winding down towards Florence. It became a popular haunt for tourists seeking cooler air; Gertrude Stein and Alice Toklas spent a summer there; and many modern tourists follow them today. Fiesole then is just one of many examples of a town that was Etruscan, becomes Roman, then becomes Tuscan, both in the Renaissance sense and in the sense of somewhere which encapsulates what we think of as a typically Tuscan scene, with its cypresses and hills and piazzas and sunshine.

The excellent local museum covers the full range of material through to medieval, but the Etruscan material dominates, as in almost every archaeological museum in Tuscany. Periodization is inevitable, and it is unsurprising what is the main draw; the 'mysterious' Etruscans have it over the rather boring Romans every time. Yet that bath, temple, and theatre complex tells us something important about the construction of a municipal life in Faesulae, and its continuity.

Some families did survive the upheaval described at the end of Chapter 9. The Caecina family at Volterra managed to survive Sulla, Caesar, and Augustus, and were commemorated on the grand theatre. There were even some who survived the Perusine massacre in 40 BC; P. Volumnius A. f. Violens and L. Proculeius A. f. Titia gnatus were *quattuorvir* and *duovir*; they held the first office before the massacre and the second in the Augustan resettlement. The Seii were doing well at Volsinii until one member, Sejanus, who had been Tiberius' right-hand man, fell so foul of the emperor that he was killed and his body dragged through the streets of Rome. The disappearance of these evocative names from the epigraphic record is suggestive of a decline, but it is also based on an argument from silence. We simply do not have the information or evidence. Since epigraphy was sometimes preserved more in funerary contexts from the lower classes, we may simply be missing the records of families which continued to exist; an intriguing example of continuity is a man called Verinus, an Etruscan name, whose family tombs are in a Christian cemetery in Chiusi; we find him in Syria and celebrated as commander in a war against the Armenians in the early 4th century. Several emperors claimed Etruscan ancestors. However, families do die out, and with intermarriage, changes of name, and so forth, the old Etruscan aristocracy seems to have dwindled.

Early in the imperial period, partly as a result of the new colonies, monumental building picks up. There are aqueducts at Lucus Feroniae, Cerveteri, Falerii; bath buildings at Ferentium, Volsinii, Faesulae, and Pisa; theatres or amphitheatres at Sutrium, Ferentinum, Rusellae, Volterra, Faesulae, Florentia, and Luna. We have seen the adornment of the Forum at Tarquinia, and the continued Roman presence at Fanum Voltumnae. L. Ateius Capito built a meeting place for the local officials, a record office, an arena for watching shows, a portico, and a banquet hall at Castrum Novum. One interesting example just outside Etruria is at Ocriculum (Otricoli) with a fine theatre, amphitheatre, and nymphaeum. Many of these buildings must have been maintained throughout the empire, and the theatres and amphitheatres needed to be filled with shows, all of which cost money. So there was plenty of opportunity for entertainment and for conspicuous benefaction (euergetism).

Agriculture was again critical for the economic underpinning of any pre-industrial settlement. Grain, oil, and wine continued to be produced and distributed; in the 1st century AD, Pliny singles out the wheats of Chiusi and Arezzo, as Varro had done a century before. Recently, a glassmaking factory was found not far from Roselle in the Maremma. If anything, the intensity grew—this is the period when we do see larger estates and greater use of slaves. The villa became a critical feature of the extra-urban landscape.

Taking villa culture as a whole, a recent study which surveyed 50 villas across the region shows some coming to an end in the 2nd century AD, thus confirming the picture we have of an overall decline which is coherent with the so-called 3rd century crisis, a complex picture of slowdown, monetary problems, and unrest across the provinces. A classic example is the villa at Settefinestre near Cosa. Built in the 1st century BC, Settefinestre was highly active in oil and wine production, and very possibly belonged to the family of the Sestii whose amphorae are found across the

Mediterranean. It is possible that there was a slave quarter, but the villa is also sufficiently luxurious to allow for elegant leisure with high quality wall paintings, a colonnade or peristyle, atrium, and garden. So this is a villa which exemplified perfectly the culture of apparent leisure (*otium*, time to philosophize and write poetry and have fine banquets) and real productive activity. There is an upgrade in the early 2nd century AD—new bath buildings are added, but the productive side is also strengthened—and then the villa starts to slide into a phase of demolition and abandonment in the late 2nd and early 3rd century AD.

However, the villa of Le Colonne, which is nearby and shares enough structural details for some to have thought they were designed by the same architect, has a completely different phasing. There appears to be a break in the 1st century BC; another in the 1st century AD; and a third in the mid-3rd century. After each hiatus, however, the villa picks up, and it is still going in the 6th and 7th century AD, as is the settlement of Cosa. Cosa had a good Republican start, a solid Augustan period, and a vital Antonine phase, but in between are periods of decline. Turning the basement of the curia, where the local senate met, into a Mithraeum, looks like a pretty low moment for civic pride; but on the other hand the shrine of Bacchus seems never to have gone out of operation.

Consideration of other villas shows similar patterns; some came to a very determined close, and the early 3rd century was clearly tricky, but others continued successfully. Around Capena and Veii, there is little sign of a 3rd century crisis. The area between Tarquinia and Vulci also seems to have survived until the later imperial period. Constantine produced a decree encouraging the continuation of religious activity at Hispellum in Umbria, and allowing them to retain games there, which incidentally implies that the Fanum Voltumnae was still going strong (or had been revived). Near Cerveteri, Trajan founded a major port site called Centumcellae (now Civitavecchia). Inland his successor Hadrian built a substantial bath complex, the Terme Taurine (one of

17. 2nd century AD bath buildings near Cerveteri, showing the continued imperial investment and interest in Etruria

several 2nd century AD bath buildings), which may in fact have had an earlier Sullan phase, and which appears to have been functional when Rutilius Namatianus passed by in the 5th century—a remarkable degree of continuity (Figure 17). Elsewhere, decline was more visible. Late 2nd and early 3rd century Bologna was still prosperous, but by the mid-3rd century, both public and private building was disintegrating. In the countryside too there are signs of contraction.

There seems no question that one of the major problems was that the new agricultural practices and the kinds of ownership which existed had not encouraged careful maintenance of irrigation channels, and this led to the resurgence of a problem long held in check—malaria. The earliest indications of malaria in Italy seem related to Gravisca on the coast of the Maremma. The area developed a bad reputation; Pliny the Younger avoided it. The problem continued until recently, and it is perhaps worth noting that one of the commonest later imperial finds is African red slip ware pottery. One can be infected with malaria by being bitten by a mosquito which has previously bitten someone infected in another country. The back and forth trade to Africa where the parasite *plasmodium falciparum* was widespread may have added to problems. It has recently been estimated that malaria may have been responsible for 60 per cent of the deaths in Grosseto in the 1840s, where figures happen to exist. Age-specific mortality was unusually high in the ages 5–9 and 20–50, as well as life expectancy being poor; in other words, malaria was having a disproportionate effect on age groups who might have been expected to fight off disease. The obvious question is why Etruria, especially coastal Etruria, flourished in the archaic period, to collapse in the later empire, and the answer may well lie in the simple failure to manage water drainage. The larger estates of the later empire were run in a way which may not have encouraged care. Absentee landowners, who avoided the areas in the more dangerous periods, and reliance on relatively disposable slave labour may simply not have encouraged proactive land management. Together with the increased African connection, the conditions were perfect for a resurgence of malaria, and consequent depopulation.

This will not have been universal. In AD 416, Rutilius Namatianus returned from Rome to his province and describes his coastal route along the shore of Etruria, where his father had once held an imperial position. He finds Pisa and Volterra on good form; but Gravisca was 'oppressed by the stench of the marsh in summer' and Cosa lay abandoned, its inhabitants allegedly having fled after an infestation of rats.

A whole range of factors in the 4th, 5th, and 6th centuries were transformative. The collapse of the Roman taxation system is part of the reason why the major trading patterns between Africa and the rest of the Mediterranean ground to a halt. There was a return to local production and local consumption. 8th century landholding patterns do not have any of the huge estates of the late Roman period. The most pressing concern may have been security. After the disasters of the 6th century, the Lombardic empire, Frankish conquest, and internal disputes made defensible sites highly attractive.

Two factors emerge in the late Roman and early medieval Etruscan world. The first is the church and the second is the phenomenon of *incastellamento*, the move uphill away from lowland villas to heights, often occupied by monasteries. Already in the 4th century we begin to see the development of church architecture in the old Etruscan centres. At Bologna, the baptistery, basilica, and episcopal palace date to the late 4th and early 5th century and overlie earlier buildings; similar palaeochristian buildings are found at Lucca, and a domus underlies the centre of Pistoia. At Pisa, traces of structures from the 5th century BC to the 5th century AD are found under the medieval city, and defining its perimeter and some of its streets, so one imagines a slow transformation. By contrast, although there are Roman finds under Arezzo, the town grid is completely different. Bishoprics are established by the 5th century at Tarquinia, Rosellae, and Sovana amongst other towns. The landscape of Etruria—now Toscana—was transformed into a landscape of production within a new set of power relations. There was still an element of competition for resource between the various ecclesiastical units, which used their position to secure territorial advantage, and in time, conspicuous consumption would become a factor in the construction of the great cathedrals.

The concentration of settlement in the old core areas with the garden perimeter coming inside the city walls is common, but there were also incomplete examples, leaving two settlements (Luni and

Sarzano, Populonia and Piombino, Tarquinia and Corneto, Forum Cornelii and Imola). The difficulty of writing about this period is to find a balance and it is well illustrated by the current debate over the fall of the Roman empire—was it sudden and catastrophic, or gradual and characterized by continuity and transformation? The Tuscan countryside was not as prosperous or populous as it had been, but central Italy was still more urbanized and more in contact with its Roman past than much of western Europe, and it was still a world of towns with local administrations. Trade, industry (brick, iron, furniture, ceramics, glass), markets, often along the old Roman roads and taking advantage of Roman way stations, all continued, in the shadow of the omnipresent Roman ruins. Sites such as Spoleto in Umbria, Lucca, and Pisa found a new vocation as trading and manufacturing cities from the 7th and 8th century; many towns as early as the 6th century were beginning to mint gold coins again.

So *incastellamento* transformed the landscape by the steady shift uphill, but also probably enhanced the exploitation of resource, whilst the old towns, many of which saw decline but not abandonment, returned to popularity because of their highly defensible positions and the fundamentally city-based nature of Lombardic administration. Tuscany began to construct the landscape familiar to us today, of high, often ruinous churches and castles, and the great cities, whose medieval and subsequent architecture often overlies the Roman and Etruscan city beneath, leaving visible little more than the odd gateway, or the ancient tombs of the Etruscan necropoleis. These remains would inspire the continuing study of the Etruscans.

Chapter 12
Etruscology: its origins and development

In the 12th century, a Spanish monk told William of Malmesbury that he had seen in a cave of horrors, full of bats and bones, golden horses and riders tantalizingly out of reach across a bronze bridge over a lake, which was defended by a figure made of bronze, who struck the water with a club, and prevented them from crossing. The figure sounds like a Hercules. This Indiana Jones adventure may or may not have emerged from knowledge of the Etruscans' tombs, but they were visible on the landscape and cannot have failed to attract some interest. It is likely that looting had begun sporadically already in antiquity.

Etruscan tomb paintings had re-entered the artistic world from the late 13th century. Giotto, who lived and worked in Tuscany for much of his life, must have seen particular paintings; in style, attitude, and pose the Judas he painted for the Arena Chapel at Padua is imitative of the head of Charun in the Tomba dell'Orco at Tarquinia; whilst in the same chapel, a vignette of dancers not only shows figures dancing like Etruscans, but it has a chamber tomb in the background. The pulpit at the baptistery of Pisa, carved by Nicola Pisano in 1260, has a figure of the Virgin Mary reclining as if on an ash-urn or sarcophagus. Etruscan pottery was being discussed from the late 13th century. By the time of the Renaissance, the Etruscans provided a visual imagery for all the great artists.

This was an age of scholarship. We can see the competitive discourse of Tuscan cities as to their origins; Corneto claimed Corythus (mentioned in Virgil) and Tarquinii as predecessors, eventually choosing the latter and changing its name to Tarquinia. Vasari's grandfather became a connoisseur of Arretine pottery, from the town of Arezzo. Alberti and many others reconstructed the funerary monument of Lars Porsenna, described by Pliny, and sought his labyrinth in the complex of underground tunnels beneath Chiusi; and fascinating parallels can be drawn between the architectural designs of Alberti and da Sangallo and depictions of Etruscan buildings on a few urns. The Tuscan order, which Vitruvius mentioned, was reconstructed to inspire the voussoir arches, pilasters, and squared masonry (which would in time become deeply rusticated), and the overarching cornice, familiar from so many Renaissance palazzi.

The Renaissance was a little in love with the Etruscans, and nowhere more so than in Florence itself, where the Etruscans featured repeatedly in Medici thinking. The Etruscans were portrayed as champions of republicanism and federal action, enlightened monarchs, doughty opponents of Rome, or mystically pious. The scarce evidence permitted all these reconstructions and that was part of the attraction of the Etruscans. A Dominican friar, Annio of Viterbo, set out to profit from this—by inventing some evidence. Annio was a forger of prolific energy: he invented Etruscan inscriptions so that by translating them he could claim to prove the entirely imagined connection between Etruscan and Hebrew; he wrote his own version of Fabius Pictor's (lost) history, and he spent some time making the case for Viterbo as a cradle of civilization, connected to Hercules and Tyrrhenus (who in turn brought the Farnese family to Italy), and the Egyptians. When Pope Alexander VI visited, he was suspiciously just in time to see Annio unearth an Etruscan tomb, which had of course been prepared earlier.

Although Annio's forgeries were soon unmasked, they would not have been as popular as they were if there were not a strong appetite for such material. Vasari was on hand when in a genuine excavation the bronze statue known as the Chimaera was found. For a while, the Etruscans were everywhere.

Almost the last substantial move in this flurry of interest was the commissioning by Cosimo II de' Medici, the Grand Duke of Tuscany, of a study on the Etruscans by the Scottish scholar and swordsman Thomas Dempster, entitled *De Etruria regali* (On Regal Etruria). The work was a major piece of scholarship, and made a serious effort to make sense of the source and Etruscan inscriptions. Yet the work was never published, a victim of the growing interest in Rome, which had, through the power of the papacy, grown stronger than Florence and was attracting all the attention. The 17th century was a relatively quiet period for Etruscan studies. Remarkably, it was Dempster's overlooked manuscript that changed all that. It was rediscovered by Thomas Coke, future Earl of Leicester (1697–1759), on his youthful Grand Tour through Italy. He was only 15 when he set out, but he was well connected and already a fanatical book collector. The manuscript was shown to him by Cosimo II's grandson, the gloomy Cosimo III; it was lavishly illustrated, and republished at Coke's expense. Coke would go on to build the marvellously Palladian Holkham Hall in Norfolk, and lived with his substantial collection of books and manuscripts. The book he had sponsored was a tremendous success, and prompted serious and determined study of the Etruscans, especially at the Accademia Etrusca of Cortona.

The 18th century was a golden time of discovery, and within the terms of the available archaeological expertise it was to some degree a time of professional development. The relative ease with which Etruscan tombs could be excavated made discovery quick, and whilst Pompeii and Herculaneum may have been more spectacular, in Tuscany at any rate there was huge interest in the new evidence. Museums developed at Florence, Volterra, and Cortona. Sadly, the more interest that was generated the more uncontrolled looting went on, and untold damage was done.

This was also the moment when the study of Etruria became international. A critical role was played by the Tuscan academies. They were an odd mix; capable of arguing over language (evincing the permanent sense of superiority of any Tuscan speaker over any other speaker of Italian), medicine, natural science, or Greek pottery. Members might take to the air in the newly introduced hot air balloons whilst colleagues sang improvised verse. Visitors included Isaac Newton and Benjamin Franklin. Meanwhile, the French, British, and Germans all began to take an interest in Etruscan archaeology.

The history of excavation at Vulci is an interesting example. Napoleon's brother, Lucien, was an early excavator. The papal authorities became involved in the 1830s, but at least part of the finds discovered by Campanari found their way into a sale in London, which helped start the British Museum's collection. Encouraged by the local and highly political academic group the Società Colombaria, Alessandro François took up the investigation and uncovered the important frescos in the Tomba François, which led to new ways of relating the Etruscans to Roman history. Bonaparte again contributed to some restoration work, but François died and the frescos languished until removed by the owner of the land, Prince Torlonia. This act was regarded as vandalism, although given the state of the tomb it may have been a blessing. The frescos then found their way to the Museo Torlonia in Rome. Occasionally they come out to public view, although the 19th century copies now give a clearer idea of the originals.

The English contribution was the traveller's guide. Mrs Hamilton Gray's *Tour to the Sepulchres of Etruria* in 1839 and the much more famous *Cities and Cemeteries of Etruria* by George Dennis, in three editions, the first in 1848 and the last in 1883, dominated the market. Dennis's work is the more remarkable; detailed and beautifully written, and richly illustrated by Samuel Ainsley. He did the work for this extraordinary account in only six years, and it has always been highly influential among British scholars, not least because of its sensitivity to landscape. Dennis's readers have always loved his infectious enthusiasm for a good meal after a bit of hard sight-seeing, but that direct observation and description was a part of his understanding of how the landscape and the economy worked.

Across the same span of time, Eduard Gerhard started to collect and publish a corpus of Etruscan mirrors, a critical resource for much about Etruscan religion. Inghirami gathered the sarcophagi, using in part the library he directed at the Volterra museum. Inscriptions were collected, tombs and tomb paintings were drawn. The development of key museums in Florence, in the Museo Gregoriano Etrusco in the Vatican, and then in the state-owned Villa Giulia, reflected the interest in the archaeological material. The Villa Giulia, a stunning collection located in Pope Julius III's villa built in the 1550s, was intended to be part of a new cultural centre, in the area which had been used in 1911 for the great exhibition to celebrate 50 years of Italian unification. These developments also represented moments in the recovery of an Italian responsibility for Italian archaeological finds, after much of the material exhibited in a show in London in 1832 had been purchased by the British Museum, and the marvellous collection of Giovanni Pietro Campana, who was convicted of embezzling money from a papal museum, was lost to the Louvre and the Hermitage when it was sold in the 1860s. In Italy, the subject began to build its scholarly edifice; *Studi Etruschi* was first published in 1927, comprising the proceedings of the First National Etruscan Conference of 1926, held by the grandly titled Permanent Committee for Etruria.

Ever since then, the Etruscans have been the object of innumerable exhibitions, including blockbusters such as the one in Zurich in 1955, a series of exhibitions in the so-called Anno degli Etruschi in 1985, which also saw the Second International Conference on the Etruscans, the remarkable collection of material from Communist Bloc museums exhibited in Berlin in 1988, just a year before the fall of the Berlin Wall, and Massimo Pallottino's 1992 exhibition in Paris and Mario Torelli's Venice show of 2000–1, both of which made strong claims for the Etruscans as a European cultural force. Both these last two shows were tapping into not just the universal appeal of the Etruscans but also their northern connections with central Europe.

Conversely, the focus on objects, necessary to create the great collections, and also a product of the absence of a surviving historical record, encouraged in the study of Etruscology an obsession with typology and classification. Tiny variations in individual pottery or metal forms, the appearance of a particular form of fibula in an unexpected place, were all scrutinized to reveal human interactions which could not otherwise be recovered, and were accompanied by an intense study of a very difficult language. Etruscology as developed by the members of the Permanent Committee refined its language, but did not necessarily extend its reach; one of the legacies of Pallottino's and Torelli's great exhibitions was to try to show how the intensity of specialist research brought very direct results in historical terms.

It might be argued that the relative obscurity of the modern scholarship, mostly in Italian, the absence of the Etruscans from the regular school classroom or university seminar, and the significance of the Etruscan tourist trail has all contributed to the persistence of a description of the Etruscans as 'mysterious'. There remained room for much non-specialist popularizing. Amongst this, pride of place goes to D. H. Lawrence's *Etruscan Places*. Published after his death, this was the product of Lawrence's trip around Tuscany in 1927, when his health was failing. Lawrence found the life and vitality he was fast losing in the past, and he contrasted it with Mussolini's Italy, which he hated. His highly positive reaction to the tomb paintings in particular has been popular, and it was an easy move to contrast the organic, connected, mysterious (that word again) Etruscans with the mechanical, clunking, unimaginative Romans. It is

exactly the sort of dynamic we have seen previously. 'To the
Etruscan all was alive,' wrote Lawrence, and from precious little
evidence conjured the marvellous world of the Etruscan, fully and
graciously at home in an interconnected world. Etruscans had a
lot of sex too and were uninhibited about it, according to the
ancient sources; that appealed to Lawrence.

A more sombre and difficult encounter is that between the great
Swiss sculptor Giacometti and the Etruscans. Giacometti was
inspired by the famous bronze statue of an elongated boy, known
poetically as the shadow of the evening ('L'ombra della sera'),
which he saw in 1960. His *Walking Man* and other works pick up
the sparseness and anonymity of decontextualized sculptures.
There is a poignancy, and sometimes a terrible sense of loss, about
this conversation across time that intersects also with the erasure
of humans and humanity at Hiroshima and Nagasaki, and in
the nuclear holocaust that everyone feared was imminent. In
achieving this deep engagement with individual works of art,
Giacometti added layers of new meaning, and deepened a sense
of strangeness. That is utterly valid, and adds to our experience,
perhaps, of those mysterious Etruscans; why did they produce
statues the way they did? Yet the Etruscans were not 'mysterious'
to the Renaissance; they were fascinating in the Enlightenment,
as was Pompeii; and by the 19th century, Dennis, albeit admitting
that their language was still a mystery, looked forward to them
being as clearly known as the Egyptians, Greeks, and Romans
through the abundance of remains. The recent resurgence of
publication, including works in English, and indeed the inclusion
of the Etruscans in this series is beginning to turn the tide.
Dennis's hope may yet be fulfilled.

Further reading

The best English introductions to the Etruscans are Sybille Haynes's *Etruscan Civilization* (London, 2000), a masterly, clear, and beautifully illustrated work which summed up a lifetime of study; and G. Barker and T. Rasmussen, *The Etruscans* (London, 1998), an indispensable guide, with an extremely helpful site by site appendix with valuable practical guidance on visiting Etruscan sites. The volume *Rasenna: Storia e civiltà degli Etruschi*, part of G. Puglise Carratelli's series on Italian peoples, published in 1986, is fundamental; J. Macintosh Turfa (ed.), *The Etruscan World* (London, 2013) is now the most substantial compendium of information. M. Pallottino's *The Etruscans* (last edition, London, 1975) is still helpful, but may soon be replaced by a translation of G. Bartoloni (ed.), *Introduzione all'Etruscologia* (Rome, 2012), which will be indispensable. L. Bonfante (ed.), *Etruscan Life and Afterlife: A Handbook of Etruscan Studies* (London, 1986) is valuable. John F. Hall (ed.), *Etruscan Italy: Etruscan Influences on the Civilizations of Italy from Antiquity to the Modern Era* (Utah, 1996) is an interesting collection of essays. For a recent excellent exhibition catalogue, see Patricia S. Lulof and Iefke van Kampen (eds.), *Etruscans: Eminent Women, Powerful Men* (Zwolle, 2011) and the most up-to-date Italian catalogue is Stefano Bruni (ed.), *Gli etruschi delle città: fonti, ricerche e scavi* (Cinisello Balsamo, 2010), whilst for those with Italian, G. Camporeale *Gli Etruschi: storia e civiltà* (third edition, Turin, 2011) is a feast.

Much of the best scholarly work is in Italian and anyone who is serious about the subject will have to tackle this material in the original language. Much appears in local catalogues, or terrifyingly expensive series. Some help is offered by the newsletter *Etruscan News* and the relatively new journal *Etruscan Studies*. Although in some respects overtaken by recent discoveries, the catalogues of the 'Year of the Etruscans' in 1985 are still an important overview edited by the most significant scholars of the field; they are M. Cristofani, *Civiltà degli Etruschi*, G. Colonna, *Santuari d'Etruria*, S. Stopponi, *Case e palazzi d'Etruria*, G. Camporeale, *L'Etruria mineraria*, A. Carandini, *La romanizzazione d'Etruria*, A. Maggiani, *Artigianato artistico in Etruria*, F. Borsi, *Fortuna degli Etruschi*, P. Barocchi and D. Gallo, *L'Accademia etrusca*.

Mario Torelli's exhibition at the Palazzo Grassi was published in monumental catalogue form and translated into English as *The Etruscans* (London and New York, 2001). His own books, *La società etrusca: l'età arcaica, l'età classica* (Rome, 1987), *L'arte degli Etruschi* (Rome, 1992), and *Storia degli Etruschi* (Rome, 1998) are extremely valuable. Two of the most important Etruscologists, both pupils of Pallottino, are Mauro Cristofani (see *Scripta selecta: trenta anni di studi archeologici sull'Italia preromana*, 3 vols. (Pisa, 2001)) and Giovanni Colonna (see *Italia ante Romanum imperium: scritti di antichità etrusche, italiche e romane (1958–1998)*, 4 vols. (Pisa, 2005)).

For the debate on the origins, see now the very helpful summary by Phil Perkins, 'DNA and Etruscan identity', in P. Perkins and J. Swaddling (eds.), *Etruscan by Definition*, British Museum Press (London, 2009), 95–111.

For the Etruscan language, see G. and L. Bonfante, *The Etruscan Language: An Introduction* (Manchester, 2002), and R. Wallace, *Zikh Rasna: A Manual of the Etruscan Language and Inscriptions* (New York, 2008).

For developments in Italian prehistory, see Emma Blake and A. Bernard Knapp (eds.), *The Archaeology of Mediterranean Prehistory* (London, 2005); the Accordia Research Centre has published many excellent volumes, and two good volumes of papers are Edward Herring, Irene Lemos, Fulvia Lo Schiavo, Lucia Vagnetti, Ruth Whitehouse, and John Wilkins (eds.), *Across Frontiers: Papers in Honour of David Ridgway and Francesca R. Serra Ridgway*

(Specialist Studies on the Mediterranean 6, London, 2006) and David Ridgway, Francesca R. Serra Ridgway, Mark Pearce, Edward Herring, Ruth Whitehouse, and John Wilkins (eds.), *Ancient Italy in its Mediterranean Setting: Studies in Honour of Ellen Macnamara* (Specialist Studies on the Mediterranean 4, London, 2000).

For the Villanovan revolution and archaic Etruscan society, see Corinna Riva's *The Urbanisation of Etruria: Funerary Practices and Social Change, 700–600 BC* (Cambridge, 2010), and Corinna Riva and Nicholas C. Vella (eds.), *Debating Orientalization: Multidisciplinary Approaches to Processes of Change in the Ancient Mediterranean* (London, 2006) has important articles on how to understand the impact of eastern ideas in the broader Mediterranean. V. Izzet, *The Archaeology of Etruscan Society* (Cambridge, 2007) is a challenging essay in interpretation. On the early impact of the Greeks, D. Ridgway, *The First Western Greeks* (Cambridge, 1992) was an elegant game-changer. On the Etruscan expansion see G. Camporeale (ed.), *The Etruscans outside Etruria* (Los Angeles, 2004).

Nigel Spivey, *Etruscan Art* (London, 1997) is a useful and provocative introduction to a complex subject. Many glossy volumes contain reproductions; on tomb paintings, S. Steingraber's two magnificent volumes, *Etruscan Painting* (New York, 1986) and *Abundance of Life: Etruscan Wall-Painting* (Los Angeles, 2006) are also highly scholarly, and M. Cristofani and M. Martelli collaborated to edit three volumes, *L'oro degli Etruschi* (Novara, 1983), *I bronzi degli Etruschi* (Novara, 1986), and *La ceramica degli Etruschi* (Novara, 1987), which are sumptuous and also highly scholarly. Larissa Bonfante, *Etruscan Dress* (Baltimore and London, 2003) is authoritative. On architecture, Axel Boëthius, *Etruscan and Early Roman Architecture* (second edition, revised by Roger Ling and Tom Rasmussen, Harmondsworth, 1978) is an excellent introduction.

On religion, the field has been transformed by American scholarship, and especially Nancy Thomas de Grummond, *Etruscan Myth, Sacred History, and Legend* (Philadelphia, 2006) and de Grummond and Erika Simon (eds.), *The Religion of the Etruscans* (Texas, 2006); see also the English translation of a French original, J.-R. Jannot *Religion in Ancient Etruria* (Madison, 2005). J. MacIntosh Turfa's superb account of an obscure text, *Divining the Etruscan World: The Brontoscopic Calendar and Religious Practice* (Cambridge, 2012) covers so much ground as to be a cultural, social, economic, medical, and agricultural history in its own right.

For the Roman conquest the standard account remains W. V. Harris, *Rome in Etruria and Umbria* (Oxford, 1971); for a broader account, see Guy Bradley, Elena Isayev, and Corinna Riva (eds.), *Ancient Italy: Regions without Boundaries* (Exeter, 2007). On Romanization, the literature is now endless, but see S. J. Keay and N. Terrenato (eds.), *Italy and the West: Comparative Issues in Romanization* (Oxford, 2001) for a sensible collection.

For Etruria in the imperial period, and a wider account of Italian developments, see E. Papi, *L'Etruria dei romani: opere pubbliche e donazioni private in età imperiale* (Rome, 2000); J. Patterson, *Landscapes and Cities: Rural Settlement and Civic Transformation in Early Imperial Italy* (Oxford, 2006); and for the later period, C. Wickham, *The Inheritance of Rome: A History of Europe from 400 to 1000* (London, 2010) contains valuable material. T. W. Potter's *The Changing Landscape of South Etruria* (London, 2009) is a brilliant and readable synthesis.

Some individual sites have received attention in English; see R. Leighton, *Tarquinia: An Etruscan City* (London, 2004); Roberta Cascino, Helga Di Giuseppe, and Helen L. Patterson (eds.), *Veii: The Historical Topography of the Ancient City: A Restudy of John Ward-Perkins's Survey* (London, 2012); Kyle M. Phillips, Jr., *In the Hills of Tuscany: Recent Excavations at the Etruscan Site of Poggio Civitate (Murlo, Siena)* (Philadelphia, 1993).

On the development of Etruscology, many of the general accounts referred to above have surveys. On the reception of the Tuscan order, see James S. Ackerman, 'The Tuscan/Rustic Order: A Study in the Metaphorical Language of Architecture', *Journal of the Society of Architectural Historians* 42.1 (1983), 15–34. On Dempster, see Robert Leighton and Celine Castelino, 'Thomas Dempster and Ancient Etruria: A Review of the Autobiography and De Etruria Regali', *Papers of the British School at Rome* 58 (1990), 337–52. For a vivid if overwritten account of recent illicit antiquities trading see Peter Watson and Cecilia Todeschini, *The Medici*

Conspiracy: The Illicit Journey of Looted Antiquities, from Italy's Tomb Raiders to the World's Greatest Museums (New York, 2007). D. H. Lawrence's *Etruscan Places* has been frequently republished; for Giacometti, see Marco Fagioli, Alessandro Furiesi, Chiara Gatti, Giuseppe Marchiori, Jean-Paul Thuillier, *Giacometti et les étrusques* (Paris, 2011).

To return to a quieter time, there is no better or more evocative a guide than George Dennis's *The Cities and Cemeteries of Etruria* (third edition, London, 1883).

Index

A

Al Mina 42, 67
Alberti, Leon Battista 132
Annio of Viterbo 132
Aristodemus of Cumae 77–9
Arruns of Clusium 80–1
Assyria 37–8
Athens 2
Augustus 6, 99, 113–14, 121,
  123–4

B

Bonaparte, Lucien 134

C

Campania 1, 71–80
Capua 16
Carthage 38, 43, 76–7, 79, 83, 84,
  107–8
Chariots 45–6
Claudius (emperor) 74, 75–6,
  121, 122
Coke, Thomas, Earl of
  Leicester 133
colonization, Greek 37, 41
colonization, Roman 102, 104,
  107, 109

C

Constantine (emperor) 126
Corinth 48
Creston 10
Cumae 37, 39, 77–80
Cyprus 38, 42

D

Delphi 69, 77, 79
Demaratus 55, 72
Dempster, Thomas 133
Dennis, George 134, 137
Dionysius of Halicarnassus 9, 105

E

Etruria, Etruscans
  alphabet 14–19
  brontoscopic calendar 90, 98
  bucchero 43, 47, 50, 57–8, 62,
    67, 70, 71, 73, 75, 77
  chronology 4, 20–2
  clothing 115–21
  DNA 12
  funerary evidence 29–33, 43–6,
    53–63, 66–7, 87
  geography 4
  gods 37
  haruspices, haruspicy 91–3
  inscriptions 11, 14–19

Etruria, Etruscans (*cont.*)
  jewellery 60–3, 121
  language 3, 8–13, 14–19
  linen book 16, 96
  in Middle Ages 6, 131–2
  mirrors 56, 60–2, 87–9, 117,
    120, 135
  origins 3, 8–13
  religion 86–97
  Renaissance 6
  sex and sexuality 55, 87,
    118–20, 132
  society 3, 33–5, 43–52, 104–6
  sport 6, 43
  temples 37
  under Rome 6, 18, 98–114, 122–30
  views on afterlife 93–7
  walls 4
  warfare 65–6
Etruscan sites
  Arezzo 59, 125, 129, 132
  Blera 23
  Bologna 21, 36, 81, 127, 129
  Cerveteri (Caere) 1, 10, 25, 28,
    32, 34, 36, 38, 41–3, 45, 51,
    53–6, 64, 66, 67, 69, 77, 83, 95,
    102, 105, 108, 110–11, 121, 125,
    126–7
  Chiusi 16, 34, 51, 53, 69, 80,
    81, 89, 106, 108, 120–1, 124,
    125, 132
  Cortona 10, 133–4
  Cosa 107, 109, 125–6, 128
  Elba 40
  Fanum Voltumnae 65, 88, 103,
    106, 125, 126
  Fiesole 69, 122–3
  Gravisca 42, 65, 67–8, 106–7,
    110, 128
  Luni sul Mignone 23
  Marzabotto 29, 66, 69, 81
  Murlo 48–9
  Orvieto 34, 53, 64, 65, 66, 67,
    68, 69, 78, 83, 103

Pisa 69–70, 81, 114, 125,
    128–30, 131
Populonia 40
Pyrgi 16–17, 42, 65, 67–8, 76,
    83–4, 106, 107, 109, 110
Roselle 41, 108
San Giovenale 23
Sorgenti della Nova 23
Sovana 23, 75, 129
Spina 29, 69, 81
Tarquinia 1, 10, 22, 25, 28, 32,
    34, 36, 41–2, 44, 53–6, 59, 64,
    67, 72, 83, 89, 91–3, 95, 99,
    102, 106, 110–11, 114, 125, 126,
    129–30, 131, 132
Veii 10, 20, 21, 22, 25, 28, 31, 34,
    41, 51, 53, 54, 57, 64, 65, 67, 75,
    83, 85, 96, 100–3, 105, 106,
    114, 126
Verrucchio 36, 40
Vetulonia 41
Volsinii 16, 34, 60, 67,
    75, 83, 103, 105–6, 114,
    124–5
Volterra 1, 41, 50, 69, 95, 108,
    124, 125, 128, 133, 135
Vulci 23, 34, 41, 43, 50, 54,
    59, 60, 64, 66, 74, 90, 111,
    126, 134

F

Faliscans 101–2
France, Southern 43, 70, 81–2
Frattesina 23–4, 35

G

Gades 38
Gauls 72, 77, 80–1, 85, 100, 103–5,
    107, 108
gender 31
Giacometti, Alberto 137
gift-giving 45

Giotto 131
Gracchus, Tiberius and Gaius 111–12

H

Hadrian (emperor) 126–7
Hamilton Gray, Mrs. 134
Hannibalic War 107–8
Herodotus 8–13, 42, 67
Hieron of Syracuse 79
Holkham Hall 133
Horses 45–6
huts, houses 31–5

I

incastellamento 129–30
Indo-European language 13–19

J

Julius Caesar 6, 73, 88, 91,
    113–14, 124

L

Lars Porsenna 78, 90, 132
Lawrence, D. H. 136–7
Lemnos 11
Livia, wife of Augustus 121
Lydians 8–13

M

Macedonia 3
Maecenas 6, 121
malaria 127–8
Mycenaean, Mycenaeans 14, 23,
    25, 38, 41, 46

N

Naukratis 67–8
Nigidius Figulus 90

O

Olympia, Olympic Games 42, 43
Otricoli (Ocriculum) 125

P

Pallottino, Massimo 11, 136
Pelasgians 9–13
Perugia 18, 69, 108, 113
Phoenicians 4, 37–43
Pithecusae 39

R

roads, Roman 110–11
Rome 2, 68, 71–5
Romulus and Remus 72

S

Samnites 80, 103–4
Sarcophagus of the Spouses,
    Cerveteri 56, 95
Sardinia 42, 43
Seiantia Hanunia Tlesnasa 121
Servius Tullius 72–3, 75
Social War 111–13
Spain 42–3, 76
Spina 69, 81
Spurinna family, Tarquinia 99

T

Tarquinius Priscus 72, 75
Tarquinius Superbus 73
Terramare culture 22
Thefarie Velianas 16
Theopompus of Chios 118–20
Tiber 41, 100–4
Torelli, Mario 136
Trajan (emperor) 126
Troy, Trojan War 9, 10, 46–7,
    56, 100

Index

U

Urgulania 121

V

Vibenna, Aulus and Caelius 74–5
villa culture 125–7

Villa Giulia Museum 135
Villanovan culture 21,
        25–35

W

Wedgwood, Josiah 36
William of Malmesbury 131

CLASSICS
A Very Short Introduction
Mary Beard and John Henderson

This Very Short Introduction to Classics links a haunting temple on a lonely mountainside to the glory of ancient Greece and the grandeur of Rome, and to Classics within modern culture – from Jefferson and Byron to Asterix and Ben-Hur.

'The authors show us that Classics is a "modern" and sexy subject. They succeed brilliantly in this regard ... nobody could fail to be informed and entertained – and the accent of the book is provocative and stimulating.'

John Godwin, *Times Literary Supplement*

'Statues and slavery, temples and tragedies, museum, marbles, and mythology – this provocative guide to the Classics demystifies its varied subject-matter while seducing the reader with the obvious enthusiasm and pleasure which mark its writing.'

Edith Hall

CLASSICAL MYTHOLOGY
A Very Short Introduction
Helen Morales

From Zeus and Europa, to Diana, Pan, and Prometheus, the myths of ancient Greece and Rome seem to exert a timeless power over us. But what do those myths represent, and why are they so enduringly fascinating? This imaginative and stimulating *Very Short Introduction* is a wide-ranging account, examining how classical myths are used and understood in both high art and popular culture, taking the reader from the temples of Crete to skyscrapers in New York, and finding classical myths in a variety of unexpected places: from Arabic poetry and Hollywood films, to psychoanalysis, the bible, and New Age spiritualism.

www.oup.com/vsi

SOCIAL MEDIA
Very Short Introduction

Join our community

www.oup.com/vsi

- Join us online at the official Very Short Introductions **Facebook** page.
- Access the thoughts and musings of our authors with our online **blog**.
- Sign up for our monthly **e-newsletter** to receive information on all new titles publishing that month.
- Browse the full range of Very Short Introductions online.
- Read **extracts** from the Introductions for free.
- Visit our library of **Reading Guides**. These guides, written by our expert authors will help you to question again, why you think what you think.
- If you are a teacher or lecturer you can order inspection copies quickly and simply via our website.

ONLINE CATALOGUE
A Very Short Introduction

Our online catalogue is designed to make it easy to find your ideal Very Short Introduction. View the entire collection by subject area, watch author videos, read sample chapters, and download reading guides.